EXECUTIVE DIRECTORS GUIDE

The Guide for Successful Nonprofit Management

Written by:
Deborah Linnell
Zora Radosevich
Jonathan Spack
Third Sector New England, Boston, MA

Published by:
United Way of Massachusetts Bay

Acknowledgments

We would like to thank the many nonprofit organizations and leaders who helped us frame the scope and content of the Guide through their willingness to respond to surveys, serve on our Practitioners Advisory Group, review chapters and provide other expertise or assistance as needed. In particular, we would like to thank Martha Breunig, Ray Considine, Deborah DeBare, Diane D'Errico, Joanne Donoghue, James Earley, Jim Haskell, Karen Jeffreys, Kathy Jellison, Bruce MacDonald, Denise K. Maguire, Francine Mantak, John Pearson, Charlotte Ryan, Bob Sable, Surl Silberman, Joyce Strom, Jon Thompson, and Judith E. Wise, CGSE.

Finally, we would like to thank Marilyn Anderson Chase and Carlos Martinez of the United Way of Massachusetts Bay for making this Guide possible.

Deborah Linnell
Zora Radosevich
Jonathan Spack

Published by

THIRD SECTOR
New England

Third Sector New England
18 Tremont Street, Suite 700, Boston, MA 02108
www.tsne.org

Printed in the United States of America

ISBN 0-9717426-0-X

How To Use This Guide

The idea for this Guide came from Marilyn Anderson Chase of the United Way of Massachusetts Bay, who has faithfully carried her copy of the United Way's 1981 Executive Directors guide with her from job to job for nearly 20 years. Needless to say, much has changed in the world of nonprofit management since 1981, and we were excited to have the opportunity to share our own cumulative learning with others. But we also wanted to retain the spirit of the earlier edition by making this version relevant and user-friendly, especially for less-experienced practitioners.

Each chapter is written to stand alone, but all are linked by a philosophy which emphasizes stakeholder participation in vision creation, strategy development, and decision-making. So you can start almost anywhere, although you may want to skim through the whole book first to see what captures your interest.

We hope you will find this Guide to be a useful tool as you work to create and sustain healthy, effective organizations and communities, and partner with colleagues to build a robust, self-confident nonprofit sector.

Deborah Linnell
Zora Radosevich
Jonathan Spack

Third Sector New England, Boston, MA
June, 2001

Table of Contents

LEADERSHIP

"The best leaders operate in four dimensions: vision, reality, ethics, and courage. . . The real challenge of leadership is to develop all four of these often-contradictory modes of thinking and behaving at once."

– Philosopher Peter Koestenbaum, interview in Fast Company, March 2000

CHAPTER 1

A Four-Step Approach

Participatory, Partnership-Based Leadership

Keeping Your Balance

Strategies for Maintaining Your Balance

So much has been written on the subject of leadership (including, inevitably, *Leadership for Dummies*), that to try to cover the topic comprehensively in one, brief chapter is an impossible task. (A recent article in the *Harvard Business Review* asserts that 2,000 books on leadership were published in 1999). So we won't try. Instead, we address what we believe are the critical leadership issues for executive directors of nonprofit organizations, including:

- demystifying the concept of leadership and presenting a simple model for understanding it;
- stimulating readers to think about their own leadership competencies and styles;
- encouraging self-reflection; and
- making a case for participatory, partnership-based leadership, where decision-making authority is distributed throughout the organization.

To give you an idea of the range of opinion on this topic, consider these opposing quotes from two noted authors:

"Vision is the commodity of leaders, and power is their currency."

– Warren Bennis, author of numerous books on leadership

"The belief that crafting the vision is primarily a leadership-at-the-top function defeats, right at the beginning, the intent of driving ownership and responsibility toward those close to the work..."

– Peter Block, consultant and author (Flawless Consulting, The Empowered Manager, Stewardship)

A Four-Step Approach

Unlike many of the subjects covered in this guide, leadership can't be learned from a book. Effective leadership is in large part a matter of personal values, choices, commitments, and characteristics – tempered by experience. Much as we would like to believe otherwise, not everyone has what it takes to be a leader. However, if you have the right raw material to begin with, it is possible to become a better leader by reading and reflecting on the latest research and best thinking on the subject and by putting into practice the ideas that resonate for you.

We suggest a four-step approach to leadership enlightenment and growth:

1 Define it for yourself. The above quotes from Bennis and Block offer radically different views of leadership. In fact, Block eschews the word altogether, preferring the more democratic "stewardship." The way you envision your role as executive director (your "mental model") shapes everything you do, from your relationship with your board, staff, and funders to the way your budget is put together; even the physical layout of your office space can be affected by the way you think of your role in relation to other staff and the organization as a whole.

Do you have a clear enough mental model of your role as a leader to write it down in one or two declarative sentences? Try it here:

My role as the leader of my organization is to

____

____

____

____

Was it hard to do? Was your description closer to Bennis or Block? We admit to a bias; we are strong believers in the stewardship model articulated by Peter Block. We think it's the model best suited to twenty-first-century realities where the ability to adapt and make rapid responses to change will be a necessity for every organization's survival. It is very difficult for an organization to be flexible and adaptable if power and decision-making are concentrated at the top, no matter how open-minded the person at the top may be.

Evaluate yourself. As a leader, where do you fall on the spectrum of styles and characteristics? How do you even know what this spectrum looks like? A great deal of information is available to anyone with the time to immerse himself or herself in the literature. We recommend taking the Myers-Briggs Personality Inventory, the Learning Styles Inventory or some other assessment tool. Read some of the scores of books on leadership.

A study[1] conducted by the consulting firm Hay/McBer identifies six distinct leadership styles and analyzes their effectiveness in creating a positive working environment and yielding good financial results. The following table presents the chief characteristics of the six styles of leadership.

Leadership Style	Chief Characteristic
Authoritarian	Demands compliance
Affiliative	Creates harmony, builds emotional bonds
Democratic	Forges consensus through participation
Authoritative	Mobilizes people towards a vision
Pacesetting	Sets high standards for performance
Coaching	Develops people for the future

According to the study, the authoritative, affiliative, democratic, and coaching styles were considered effective in promoting a positive work environment and yielding good financial results. The best leaders were those who had mastered all six of these styles and could draw on any one of them when appropriate. The *key point* is that good leaders can adjust their leadership style as needed and are sensitive to the impact they are having on others.

Another Perspective on Leadership Qualities

Another perspective on leadership qualities was recently offered by Robert Goffee and Gareth Jones[2], who claim to have identified four qualities that define inspirational leadership. Their work, which assumes that the basic elements of vision, authority, energy, and strategic direction are already present, concludes that inspirational leaders:

- selectively show weakness in order to establish trust and authenticity (Authors' note: the reality of gender bias suggests to us that this strategy will work better for male leaders than for female leaders.);
- use instinct and intuition to sense the appropriate timing and course of actions;
- use "tough empathy," by which they mean balancing respect for the individual with respect for the task at hand; and
- demonstrate unique qualities to create the distance necessary for effective motivation of others.

Make a choice. Ask yourself what kind of leader you want to be. Ask what style of leadership will help you grow as a person and help your organization reach toward its mission and vision. Develop a vision for yourself as a leader and commit yourself to working toward it. Remember the fundamental rule: you must be authentic to be an effective leader in the long term. If you try to emulate someone else, even one of the many leaders who have written books describing their own wonderful successes, you will be heading in the wrong direction.

[1]The Study, conducted by the consulting firm Hay/McBer, was analyzed in Daniel Goleman's article *"Emotional Intelligence," Harvard Business Review,* March-April 2000. The table was drawn from information presented in the same article.

[2]See Goffee, Robert and Jones, Gareth, "Why Should Anyone Be Led by You?" *Harvard Business Review,* (September-October 2000): 63-70.

Create a plan and put it to work. Make a step-by-step plan of what you must do to realize your vision of leadership. Try not to censor your own thinking. Here are a few ideas to use in developing your plan, but remember, each element in the plan should move you towards the leadership vision you have articulated for yourself:

- Listen more and talk less.
- Take a vacation.
- Take a course on financial management.
- Immerse yourself in the leadership literature.
- Share information – and the nitty-gritty details of your decision-making process – with other staff members more regularly.
- Take more interest in the opinions – and problems – of your coworkers.
- Delegate more tasks.
- Find a job that is a better fit for you.
- Take strong action on that long-standing board or personnel matter that's been causing you to lose sleep.
- Learn to control your anger.
- Learn to let your anger out.

Whatever elements your plan contains, be sure to include peer support and plenty of feedback. Peer networking offers an invaluable learning tool for executive directors. If you don't have a peer network or can't find one to join, start one! It's easy. Just call two or three colleagues whom you trust and respect (and from whom you think you can learn something), and ask them to join you once a month for a discussion among peers. Make it a priority. Block out a couple of hours on a regular basis to meet and provide support for one another. Use the time to share fears, fantasies, problems, successes, and resources for learning. If you think you are too busy to do this, consider whether your work style will serve you and your organization well in the long term.

Participatory, Partnership-Based Leadership

We believe that the leadership style best suited to nonprofit organizations regardless of size is one based on the partnership model. In an important sense, we are fortunate as nonprofit leaders. We don't have to grapple with what philosopher Peter Koestenbaum describes as a major paradox for business leaders: how to preserve human values while coping with a "brutal business reality." Sure, we have to pay careful attention to the bottom line and make tough, sometimes painful decisions, but our mission is what drives us. We do not have to choose between valuing profit and valuing people.

Third-sector organizations exist to make communities better places for people to live, not to maximize the income of their shareholders. Therefore, we believe nonprofit organizations should adopt organizational models consistent with a focus on people rather than profit.

People-centered systems and practices can and do work well in nonprofit organizations, community-based organizations in particular. Organizational models based on partnerships among board, staff, and other stakeholders hold true to the values we espouse. Ironically, in pursuit of management efficiency, many in the third sector have looked to the for-profit business sector for models. This approach, when it discounts the human values on which most nonprofits are founded, often results in a disconnect between mission and internal practices, creating staff dissatisfaction, turnover, and ultimately alienation of the organization from those it exists to serve.

If the participatory or partnership model resonates with you, we recommend *Stewardship* by Peter Block as a starting point for your learning. Block defines stewardship as "giving order to the dispersion of power," which means that people throughout the organization have the power to determine how they do their work. Participatory or partnership leadership is based on a rejection of the paternalistic premise that the people at the top *know best.* If you can lead without being in total control, are comfortable in an environment of shared power and responsibility, and think your board and staff will support this approach – not everyone *wants* power, after all, because it entails accountability – then we urge you to consider embracing a participatory or partnership model of leadership.

The Four Requirements of True Partnership[3]

1 Exchange of purpose: Everyone, at all levels, is responsible for defining organizational purpose (mission, vision, and values) through dialogue.

2 Right to say no: Partnership does not mean that you always get what you want. You may lose your argument, but you never lose your voice.

3 Joint accountability: Everyone is responsible for outcomes and for the current reality. The price of the freedom that partnership offers is personal accountability for success and failure.

4 Absolute honesty: In a partnership, not telling the truth to each other is an act of betrayal.

The Nine Principles for Stewardship-based Governance[4]

1 Maximize the choice for those closest to the work. Put decision-making authority where the work gets done.

2 Reintegrate the managing and the doing of the work. Management becomes a set of tasks, not a job title. Everyone manages, although some have a wider perspective, and everybody does work that adds value for constituents.

3 Let measurement and controls serve the core workers. Use team and peer agreements to design evaluation tools and maintain control. Measure results and outcomes, not behavior and style.

4 Yield on consistency across groups and support local solutions. Encourage unique solutions whenever possible.

5 Service is everything. Definitions of roles and decisions about services and evaluations all emerge from dialogue with customers and coworkers. Bosses are suppliers, not customers.

6 Deglorify management as a job title and demystify staff functions. Managers exist only to add value to the core work.

7 End secrecy. Full disclosure of business information should be the rule. The more sensitive the issue, the more it needs to be talked about. Full disclosure includes individual responsibility for communicating.

8 Demand a promise. In return for increased freedom of choice, everyone must make a commitment to act only in the best interests of the whole organization.

9 Redistribute wealth. Design the compensation system so that everyone's pay is tied to the success of the team, department and entire organization. Eliminate automatic increases.

Keeping Your Balance

Most of us have chosen to work in the nonprofit sector because of strongly held personal values. For many third-sector leaders, however, this very passion can result in an unhealthy imbalance between work and personal life that can have major personal and organizational consequences. The more closely your personal values match your organization's mission, the more vulnerable you are to blurring, or even obliterating, the line between home and work. The more time you spend working, the more you shortchange your family, your friends, and, not least, yourself.

Over time, all those night meetings, weekends at the office, and abbreviated vacations will take their toll. The result can be *burnout,* which, in turn, may lead to a voluntary or involuntary departure, creating a potentially major disruption for your organization, not to mention personal and professional anguish.

The secondary effects of this nonprofit workaholic syndrome can be dangerous, too. If the executive director expects other staff to work the same long hours, week after week, that he or she does, low morale and high turnover are likely to be the outcome. Moreover, this set of expectations fosters a culture of crisis management rather than one that values strategic thinking and reflection.

[3]Block, Peter. *"Stewardship"* San Francisco: Berrett-Koehler Publishers, 1993.

[4]Ibid

Strategies for Maintaining Your Balance

Sixteen years ago, a small group of executive directors in the Boston area created an informal support group that came together for monthly meetings. Of the nine people who have been members at one time or another, only one is still an executive director. The others have moved on, quite happily, to other management-level jobs. So, we weren't surprised at the results of a recent survey of executive directors conducted by the Support Center of San Francisco, now Compasspoint. Although it did not use a scientific sample, the study, entitled *Leadership Lost,* found that *only 20 percent* of the group would take another job as executive director.

We believe the principal reason for this phenomenon is stress-induced burnout. If you are doing work you are passionate about, stress and emotional fatigue are likely to affect you sooner or later. While you probably can't avoid these consequences entirely, you can prevent them from completely undoing you by setting reasonable limits for yourself and sticking to them. Here are a few strategies that have worked for executive directors we know:

- Prioritize and delegate. Separate out the things that only you can do from those that others can do. Build in 30 minutes of planning time each day for organizing your work around these priorities.
- Work toward a flatter organizational structure. The more that power and responsibility are dispersed throughout the organization, the less the burden will fall on your shoulders.
- Set and stick to reasonable limits on your work hours. (For example, be out of office by 6:00; don't work at home after 8:00; and don't exceed four hours on the weekend.)
- Spend your personal time doing things that are different from your work tasks. (For example, if you spend a great deal of time in meetings during the day, limit the number of home-based activities you do that involve meetings.)
- Improve the aesthetics of your work space.
- Find someone outside of work to whom you can vent and gripe. Form or join a support group or arrange a regular meeting time with a trusted colleague.
- Nurture strong commitments to family, friends, and nonwork interests. It is easier to say "no" to more work if you have said "yes" to a personal life.
- Consider a personality-type analysis to help you focus on the parts of your job you enjoy and try to do more of them.
- When you travel, try to maintain your personal rhythms for exercise, sleep, and reasonable work hours.

Good luck! Remember the old axiom: No one ever went to their grave wishing they had spent more time at the office.

MISSION
VISION
VALUES

CHAPTER 2

This may be the shortest chapter in the guide, but it is probably the most important. Executive directors are the "lead missionaries" for their organizations. This chapter focuses on the challenges involved in sustaining the mission, vision, and values that give meaning and relevance to an organization.

Mission, vision, and values are important words that express the guiding principles and aspirations of an organization. Because they are so important to the working of the organization, we will start with some definitions. In this guide:

- *Mission* describes the overarching purpose of the organization – the reason it exists.
- *Vision* is the picture of the future that the organization seeks to create. Holding a vision helps us decide which strategies to implement in actualizing our mission.
- *Values* are our beliefs in action – they guide our behavior as we take action to realize our vision and purpose.

When mission, vision, and values are aligned, they can be articulated and practiced by everyone inside the organization because they are clear and consistent. Those outside the organization can recognize them because they are evident in everything the organization does, from the way the phone is answered and clients are treated to the way fundraising is conducted and board meetings are run.

Expiring Words on Paper or Daily Inspiration?

The job of the board and the executive director is to use the mission as a screen for every major organizational decision. Many executive directors and board members revisit the mission only during an annual retreat or strategic planning session. They spearhead a great deal of good work during those brief hours, write a lot of words on paper, and sometimes even type up the meeting notes. And then they wait until the next session to revisit the same old work. Rarely is a plan made for actualizing the mission, vision, and values of the organization on a daily basis.

The new work of the executive director and the board is to set the stage for holding the mission, vision, and values at the forefront of the minds of everyone associated with the organization. The executive director must reinforce these ideas on a day-to-day basis for the staff, clients, and the public. In addition, the executive director, in partnership with the board, must build relationships within the greater community to make sure that the mission of the organization still has relevance to the community and to act as lead change agent if the mission becomes outdated.

Building a mission focus within the organization is important work for the executive director. It is hard work, but it is necessary work because:

- Mission focus gives clarity to staff and other key stakeholders about why they are there;
- Vision work give staff and other stakeholders a positive understanding of where they are going; and
- Values work gives staff and other stakeholders the parameters within which they can act as they work toward making the vision a reality.

Executive directors should examine their own practices toward building a mission focus within the organization.

- Do not take the job if you do not have passion for the mission of the organization; the job of executive director is too hard not to have your heart in it.
- Do not hire *anyone* into the organization, for any job, who does not understand and have empathy for the mission.
- Develop a mission screen and values screen for all major decisions for the organization.
- Use the mission screen and values screen when hiring; make it clear to prospective employees that they will be expected to understand, support, and uphold the mission and values of the organization.

- Ask the board development committee to create a mission and values screen to be used when considering prospective board members.
- Consider staff and board adherence to mission and values during evaluations; be clear about the consequences of not supporting the mission and values of the organization.
- Incorporate the mission and vision screens into fundraising activities; develop a policy that requires a review of proposed fundraising techniques in light of mission and values.
- Incorporate the same screens in all program development actions.

A *mission screen* can be as simple as designing a set of questions that the staff or board should ask in order to test whether a job or board candidate or organizational activity is aligned with the mission and values of the organization. (See **Keeping the Mission, Vision, and Values Alive** later in this chapter.)

Keeping it simple is a good idea when you are working to keep your mission and values at the forefront. Clarity and consistency are most important in articulating these ideas, both inside the organization and outside, to constituents and the greater community.

A key role of the executive director is to serve as a model of consistency and clarity by bringing your committed belief in the mission and values of the organization to every decision and interaction that you have with each staff person, board member, volunteer, client, constituent, and member of the greater community. Seek opportunities to share your thinking and process of decision-making with members of the staff and board.

Aligning Mission and Values

It is easiest to start the work of aligning mission and values within your first six months on the job when you are still considered a newcomer. The following steps, however, can be followed at any time by any executive director. We encourage experienced executive directors to take time to redefine their commitment to achieving this alignment.

- *Take stock of the mission, vision, and values* of the organization through interviews with staff and clients. If you are new to the organization, take advantage of the goodwill and flexibility you have during the first few months on the job by talking to as many people as you can to get as complete a view as possible. If you are taking over a troubled agency, your first step will be to create a strategy to put out the fires, but also take time to begin talking with people, individually and in teams. If you have been on the job for some time, you may want to hire a consultant to facilitate the process or conduct the interviews.
- *Gather information and take stock of the employees.* Ask people to tell their stories about what attracts them to the agency, whether and why they choose to participate in decision-making processes, and what their vision is for themselves and for the organization. Hold as many *informal* one-on-one conversations as you can manage, keeping in mind that the more you can hold, the better. If you are new, your first three months on the job may be the only window of objectivity that you have; past this point, you will likely be too much a part of the system to be able to have an objective lens with which to view the agency. (See the Appendix of this guide for a sample organizational assessment tool.)
- *Introduce yourself to key stakeholders,* and ask them what they think about the organization's mission, strategies, and vision. If you cannot articulate the mission clearly, ask stakeholders what they think the vision and strategies should be.
- *Bring people together* to define the organizational vision and values. If you are new to the organization, try to do this within your first six months.

We have included several exercises in the appendix to help groups visualize the future, agree to a set of values, and begin to achieve mission focus. Many consultants are available who can facilitate a retreat session using exercises like these. Because establishing alignment of mission and values is usually considered the first step in organizational development work, many funding sources exist for technical assistance that can help pay for a consultant to assist you. If consultant help is not available, the executive director or a board member can run the retreat and facilitate the group exercise.

Keeping the Mission, Vision, and Values Alive

Keeping the mission, vision, and values alive in your organization is so central to its operations that virtually every chapter in this guide will address it at some level. The key point is to use your mission and values screens for all major organizational decisions and to periodically renew the organizational vision for the future.

Keep the mission alive by referring to it often and encouraging everyone in the organization to use it as a screen in all areas of organizational decision-making by asking questions such as:

- Is this activity consistent with our mission?
- Is this collaboration getting us closer to our mission?
- Is this funding source or practice moving us towards or away from our mission?
- Does this board nomination process and staff screening process ensure that candidates are aligned with our mission?

Revisit values periodically. At the very least, revisit values during an annual retreat or strategic planning process. Even better, encourage regular discussion and reinforcement of organizational values as part of general staff meetings. Periodically pose the following questions:

- Does our behavior with each other reflect the values-in-action that we want to demonstrate?
- Does our behavior and attitude toward the people using our services reflect our values?
- Is our regard for the community reflected in our values?
- How would we orient a new staff person to our expectations about value-driven behaviors in our organization?
- What are the consequences in our workplace when our values are not upheld?

One option for holding people accountable to the expectations within the organization for value-driven behaviors is to incorporate questions about values into evaluation forms and processes. Another option is to write an organizational code of ethics.

Periodically hold conversations among the staff and other stakeholders that ask:

- How has the organization acted and looked in the past?
- What might it look like in the future if we disregarded our mission and values?
- How are staff treated?
- How are clients treated?
- Have we been honest with funders?
- Have we chased inappropriate funding?
- Have we picked the wrong partners for collaboration?

It may be difficult to discuss past dysfunction openly. However, it is possible to begin a healing process by finding a way to tell the story from as many perspectives as possible, as honestly as possible, and through the screen of how the organization collectively (rather than individually) fell away from its mission and values.

The key point is that mission, vision, and values should not be relegated to a once-a-year visit at a formal retreat or planning session. Keep the mission, vision, and values alive and watch the organization come alive as well.

PROGRAM DEVELOPMENT

CHAPTER 3

Programs are the strategies nonprofit organizations use to fulfill their mission. All other organizational functions, including executive direction, planning, fundraising, financial management, and people management *are merely supports to program development.* The best organizations, of course, balance relevant programs with sound management practices, but program development comes first.

Nonprofit executives and managers would do well to keep in mind the "12 Step" programs of Alcoholics Anonymous and its offspring. Employing no staff and with virtually no overhead, these member or constituent-driven programs are focused deeply on mission, principles, values, and a few simple program tenets. By staying focused on their mission and program, 12 Step programs have had remarkable outcomes and have helped countless people.

Sometimes, management focuses so much on fundraising and managing people that it loses its focus on mission and program. In this chapter we suggest an approach that focuses on mission and program, while maintaining discipline and innovation in management functions, in order to lead nonprofit organizations to better outcomes for participants, greater employee and board stewardship of mission, and increased funding.

The Heart of the Nonprofit Organization

An executive director's job is to ensure that programs relate deeply to the mission and to the real needs of constituents and the community. *Programs should follow need, not money.*

Doing programs right takes guts, smarts, and the knowledge that no agency, executive director, or board can do it alone. Starting and sustaining programs that yield positive outcomes for constituents and community can mean having the integrity to avoid getting caught up in the vicissitudes of the funding world. Good programs always start with vision and are followed by hard work. They often require courage.

In smaller organizations, executive directors will be doing the visioning, planning, testing of ideas with constituents, fundraising and, often, implementation of new programs. It is up to them to involve as many stakeholders as possible in the development, evaluation, and retooling of new programs.

In larger nonprofits, executive directors are responsible for:

- facilitating stakeholder ownership and input into program development;
- ensuring that the mission is used as a filter for new programs;
- strategically intertwining the support functions of budgeting, staffing, funding, and ongoing evaluation into program development; and
- communicating to various public groups the program's purpose, as well as hoped-for final outcomes and success (or lack of) as initial results begin to emerge.

Characteristics of Good Programs

Nonprofit leaders and stakeholders must work together to determine criteria for developing and evaluating good, effective programs for their own organizations. There are, however, some universal characteristics of good programs that executive directors should keep in mind.

Good programs:

- further the mission of the nonprofit;
- meet documented needs of the nonprofit's core constituents;
- are meaningful to stakeholders, including board, staff, community, and funders;
- are cost-effective;
- provide models for replication by other organizations;

- have open feedback mechanisms that enable stakeholders to provide constructive criticism that leads to improvement or retooling when necessary; and
- end when they are no longer useful.

Envisioning, Designing, and Starting Good Programs

In the heyday of the 1970s and early 1980s, if you had a good idea and could write a short proposal, a local foundation or individual was likely to fund it. A nonprofit organization would hire people and run the program, usually collecting few, if any, statistics on usage and rarely doing any formal evaluation. Much of the nonprofit programming that we take for granted today was developed "in the old days" on a wing and a prayer; community health centers, citizen action groups, substance abuse programs, community development corporations, legal services, job training programs, adult education, domestic violence programs, and homeless shelters were envisioned and built by politically savvy nonprofit leaders who then worked with local legislators and Congress to create larger public funding streams.

This success at garnering public money changed everything. Public money rightfully brought demands for public accountability. Gone were the days when nonprofit staff were viewed automatically as "doing good." Public perception was damaged by too many nonprofits that were poorly run or had become mere "fundraising machines."

Today, nonprofits have to earn their stripes. Programs have to be carefully designed to withstand the scrutiny of consumers, funders, and the public. This is not a negative. While it makes our work harder, it also makes us more accountable and more likely to develop programs that are better and more responsive than the programs of old. Our challenge is to remember to whom we are accountable and why the programs exist in the first place.

15 Steps to Program Design in an Era of Accountability

The following, *not-necessarily-linear steps* will help you design new programs that meet the test of accountability to stakeholders.

1. Engage the staff and board in an ongoing conversation and learning mode about the organization's field of work. New ideas and vision often emerge from informal conversations with colleagues and meeting with peers to tackle problems. Encourage people to question and critique current programs and practices, keeping in mind the underlying question: *How can we do better?*

2. Create dialogue opportunities with constituents and the community to get and test ideas and vision. Use community feedback to begin to focus a "good idea" into program purpose and concrete goals. Use community feedback to define what the outcomes of a particular program initiative should be; it may be quite different from what staff feel the outcomes should be.

3. Research whether similar programs exist in other parts of the city, state, or country. Gone are the days of developing a program in a vacuum or duplicating a service offered nearby.

4. Design the activities that will flow from each goal and lead to hoped-for outcomes, making sure to base them on research and feedback from end users.

5. Chart the staffing pattern and needs related to the program.

6. Describe the impact of the program on the whole agency. Include the impact on staff time, equipment usage, office space, supplies, and staff training budgets.

7. Build the program budget as realistically as possible, including personnel, space, and other indirect costs.

8. Outline the concept of the program initiative and begin to introduce it to other stakeholders, including funders, policy makers, peers in other agencies, and colleagues. Gather feedback, look

for synchronicity, note potential for collaboration, and ask everyone to suggest who might be interested in funding the concept.

9. Identify funding sources, including internal funds if the agency can afford to front the start-up costs for a program it urgently wants to get underway.

10. Approach funding sources.

11. Develop evaluation tools, feedback loops and/or learning moments, and places for conversations that will help determine if the program is doing what it set out to do and measure outcomes for participants.

12. Write out the steps and timeline for the program's start-up.

13. Implement.

14. Evaluate. Ask yourselves: We did all this work; for what?

15. Improve.

In small nonprofits, the executive director will be involved in almost every one of these steps. In new and emerging nonprofits, the executive director (and board of directors when there isn't an executive director) will do everything, from soup to nuts, including implementation.

In large and mid-sized nonprofits, program managers and line staff will help with many of these steps, and the executive director will focus more on facilitating program development and ensuring quality of conversations, concepts, program start-up, and program efficacy.

Case Study: From Job Training to Economic Development

Over the years, a Boston area community development corporation (CDC) had evolved into an organization that focused almost solely on housing needs, despite its mission charge to work on economic development as well. A couple of years ago, one board member suggested that the organization submit a proposal for a state grant for a welfare-to-work job training program. The time line was short, but the executive director agreed to turn the proposal around. The CDC received the grant and a staff person was hired to develop and run a job training program.

The program that was developed met state requirements, but was not producing many successful graduates. The proposal had been written quickly, with no time to get input from staff or constituents on the real needs of the community. The staff person grew frustrated and felt the program was not meeting the needs being articulated by attendees. In conversations with housing staff at the CDC, she found out that they, too, had recognized the need for a quality program and believed a more holistic program was needed to help struggling tenants learn to create budgets so they could meet their rent and other basic needs.

The job training staff person, with support from concerned housing staff, asked to meet with the executive director to request that they be allowed to conduct a community survey to find out what kind of job training program would work for people in the community. The executive director recognized that she had rushed into the job training program as a result of "chasing money." She felt she owed it to the staff and the community to give them a chance to retool the program into something that really worked. In giving her approval, she charged the staff with "thinking through a better mousetrap" with community input.

The staff surveyed 200 tenants of the CDC's Section 8 apartment complex. Based on the findings from the survey, they noted several areas of need that emerged from CDC constituents – including the need for English as a Second Language (ESL) training as a precursor to the job training for some residents, and the need for more financial literacy training, including work on budgeting, credit, and savings and loan issues. In addition, some constituents described the need for support in other areas of their lives, such as dealing with abusive partners, managing as a single head of- household, managing finances, and living with HIV. The staff were struck by the complexity of needs that emerged beyond the basics of "job training."

The staff created a "needs statement" based on the community feedback. They then designed program components to meet those needs. Many of the components, such as social service supports, could not be addressed by the CDC. The job training program was solid, but the staff person did not have the background needed to provide the financial literacy piece. The new program design was brought to the executive director, who worked with the team to project staffing patterns and costs. The cost of providing such a holistic approach seemed prohibitive, but she did present the staff's work to the board of directors. One board member, who worked at a local adult education center that was providing ESL classes, said he would call a meeting for interested parties from both organizations to talk about creating a partnership for providing ESL support to the CDC's job training program.

At that meeting, the executive director and staff learned that the ESL program had also found that its students needed support around family/life issues. The two executive directors decided to write a collaborative proposal to share a family services worker whose job would be to link both agencies and their constituents with local social service agencies. This family services worker would also provide basic counseling, information, referral and follow up. The idea of hiring a "social worker" type was radical for both the CDC and the ESL program – much more so for the CDC.

The job training staff person heard about an economic empowerment program that was being run in local homeless shelters and met with the staff and consultants to this program. She learned that economic empowerment classes could create a foundation for financial literacy. It would round out the "job training" program and provide personal finance information as well as help people understand their own power in creating sustainable neighborhoods and communities.

The executive director gave her approval to the job training staff person to learn the economic empowerment curriculum by taking part in a series of classes being taught at the homeless shelters. The job training staff person then adapted the curriculum to more closely match the needs of CDC's clients.

Finally, the executive director asked the staff to implement outcome measures to ensure that the retooled program was meeting the needs of consumers. She also charged the staff with doing mid-course corrections and remaining flexible in partnering with different agencies to help deliver a more holistic economic development program.

Within six months of recognizing that the job training program was not working and needed to be retooled, the following had occurred:

- Staff brought their concerns about the program to the executive director;
- The director was open to hearing constructive criticism of the program and had the self-awareness and experience to know that "chasing money" had not been in the best interest of community members or the agency;
- The executive director encouraged critical thinking and allowed it to come from many sources, including staff, community members, and the board;
- The executive director empowered the staff to take the critical thinking of others and mold this into a more responsive community program; and
- The CDC board, executive director, and staff were open to working across organizational boundaries; they partnered with a local adult education center to meet one community need and were open to learning from organizations for the homeless to meet another need.

Retooling Existing Programs

The retooling process is similar to the steps of program design discussed above. The main difference is that conversations with stakeholders can be based on actual program performance and results. Formal and informal evaluation findings and actual outcomes should be used as the basis for the next circle of learning, changing, and doing.

Effectiveness can be analyzed using formal evaluation, demographic data that describes who has been served, focus groups of people who have used the program, and informal evaluative information that staff has gleaned from participants and community members. In addition, funders or colleagues should be engaged to learn what they may know of emerging trends in the field that could influence the next generation of program design.

Nonprofits that organize themselves for continuous learning in order to create and sustain meaningful programming are sometimes called learning organizations, total quality management (TQM) organizations, or planning organizations.

Barriers to Retooling Programs

Fear of Funding Loss

Programs often stay the same simply because funding streams have not changed. Even when foundation or government funding program requirements no longer make sense, many nonprofit organizations may be reluctant to engage funders in a dialogue about change because it may result in a loss of funding. As a result, organizations maintain programs longer than their useful life because no one is willing to tell funders about the changes in the community that those on the frontlines are witnessing.

Fear of Change

Sometimes managers and line staff are worried that changing a program will reflect badly on them and make it look as if they did not know how to design a program correctly the first time. Sometimes, they simply do not want to change or learn new ways. In this new age of quick-cycle change and accountability, an increasing part of human resource work for executive directors will be recognizing and diffusing barriers that may be presented by staff who are fear-based by nature or do not like change.

Fear of True Inclusion

Another barrier to sound program design is when the "few" believe they know what is good for the "community." When there is inadequate community and consumer involvement in program design and evaluation, the result is often a program that sounds good but is not based in reality. Sometimes organizations are so invested in a program – whether intellectually, financially, or in terms of reputation, that they resist close scrutiny. As a result, change that is needed to make programs more useful to the people for whom they are intended is slow to emerge or nonexistent.

Making the Connection to Other Critical Functions

Management functions exist to support programs. Executive directors manage these functions and boards of directors provide balance and oversight – all so that line staff can implement the core programs that move the organization toward its mission.

Most of this *Executive Directors Guide* is devoted to providing insights into managing these administrative functions. In this chapter, we also provide a quick look at how a program is connected to each of the key management functions of nonprofit organizations. Each of these functions is discussed in greater detail in subsequent chapters.

Program and Strategic Planning

If the *15 Steps to Program Design* discussed previously are used for all of the organization's programs, the organization is, simply put, engaged in strategic planning. Formal strategic planning may have more steps, engage more stakeholders, and include a deeper scan of external forces working on the agency and its programs, but it is basically a system of program design on a more comprehensive scale. Strategic thinking uses a continuous circle of feedback, learning, and improving to allow program changes to occur under a quick-cycle process that responds fluidly to changes in the economy, community demographics, or technology.

Program and Constituents

In the past, programs were developed *by* charities *for* people in need. Clients, their advocates, and funders are working hard to change that pattern to one that allows more involvement from constituents in designing, implementing, and evaluating programs. Despite this effort, constituent involvement is still a missing link for many nonprofits. Lack of time, lack of belief that consumers have good ideas or understand programming requirements, and fear of true community feedback hold many organizations back from engaging with the people to whom they are most accountable.

Increased public scrutiny and the demand for accountability, however, are changing the culture of how programs are designed. Consumers of services are beginning to view nonprofit programs as businesses providing a product. They are becoming more empowered end-users. More nonprofits are working to include the voice of program participants in everything related to program design and implementation.

Program and People Practices

Society is in the midst of a transition from the industrial age, during which hierarchy was important, to the information age, in which continuous learning and reinvention is essential. Nonprofit leaders and workers who can adapt, learn, and take ownership will fare far better than those who cannot navigate change or boldly face new challenges.

Managing the complexities of helping people respond to an ever-changing environment that demands ever-changing programming is one of the greatest challenges for executive directors.

Line staff must be engaged as stakeholders and partners in carrying out the organization's mission and vision. The people actually doing the work need to be empowered to make the day-to-day decisions around program design and innovation. These decisions, in turn, must be based on demonstrable need or feedback from the community. Staff need to develop skills and tools for analyzing problems from a systems perspective. They need to be encouraged to engage in truth-telling about the organization – to be able to say what works and what does not – without fear of reprisal. Staff also need to be partners in resolving issues and cocreators of new initiatives. They need opportunities to discuss the connection between their day-to-day work and the organization's purpose and programs in order to renew their commitment and provide stewardship to the larger system.

Roles and responsibilities that have been so rigidly prescribed during the last half century will become more fluid as people work together to resolve policy, program, governance, and management issues. The "team" concept will change dramatically as agencies share staff across borders (creating interagency teams) and build complex collaborations to meet community needs.

Program and Financial Management

Many executive directors leave the issues of finance to the finance people. Executive directors do not have to be *expert* in financial management, but they should *understand the impact* that programs have on budgets, future financial projections, and the overall cost of doing business. If your financial management skills are not strong, it makes sense for you to sit down with the finance person (or team) and determine the bottom-line impact of a new program on the current budget and on future years. Include in your assessment salaries, benefits, overhead, facilities, equipment, and any new line items that a new program may incur.

Paying strict attention to the budget process provides an important reality check for executive directors eager to implement an exciting new initiative. Understand that the bottom line is the bottom line. If the money is not there and a plan is not in place to raise it, the agency must delay its start-up or reconsider whether the program can be done at all.

Closely examine the cost of doing business when taking on a government contract or foundation grant; many pay only for direct program costs, forcing the nonprofit organization to look for alternative funding for administrative and other indirect costs. If an agency has too many "direct programming only" grants, it may find itself with cash flow problems or, worse, with operating deficits and contractual obligations to fulfill – a very hard combination indeed.

Program and Fund Development

Relationships with funders are always complex, but the relationship actually gets easier when program comes first and money comes second. Good programs that are backed up by executive directors, boards, and development staff who know what they are doing will attract adequate funding – funding that doesn't dramatically change the program's intent, and doesn't pull the agency away from its mission.

The executive director's role is to ensure that program and fund development are integrally linked. Development staff should be involved in program design – the basis from which proposals develop, case statements evolve, and major donor materials emerge. Development staff should also have a link to evaluation activities in order to make reports to funders with a true understanding of a program's outcome.

Program and Public Relations

Every new program initiative needs a public relations plan. The plan should outline how the program will be promoted generally to the public and marketed to those who are the intended users of the service.

Many small and even mid-sized nonprofits believe that they simply do not have the capacity to do public relations well. Smart executive directors, however, discipline themselves to put several hours a week into this function – just as they do with fundraising tasks.

Public relations is about communication. Communication is the system that binds everything together. A little time spent on communications will help enormously with other key functions, including constituency involvement, people management, fund development, evaluation, and planning.

Program and Evaluation

In days gone by, executive directors of programs that seemed to run well and offer good services could get renewed funding and publicity with a few well-chosen anecdotes about clients whose lives had been dramatically changed. These days, there are too many organizations doing equally good work for anecdotes to tell the whole story anymore.

Anecdotes put a human face on a problem addressed by a program, but true program development demands an honest review of what works and what doesn't. For programs that are just starting up, program managers should put "process evaluation" into place to document the good, the bad, and the ugly of moving a program from idea to action. For every program, managers should define up front what the outcomes will be for participants – preferably with input from some participants themselves. Indicators that track movement toward outcomes also need to be defined. Feedback loops need to be created and maintained. Evaluation is the newest frontier for many nonprofit organizations, and *it is an absolute necessity* for those who want real information on the efficacy of their programs.

Evaluation doesn't have to be overly burdensome. A simple outcome measurement plan for a child abuse prevention program might look like this:

Outcome	Indicator	Data Collection Method
Awareness of the target audience to the signs of child abuse	Number and percentage of the target audience that can name three signs of child abuse	Telephone survey of 20 percent of those who received materials

Evaluation makes it easier for staff and others to identify programs that yield poor results. It also facilitates a revisiting of program assumptions and the retooling of program design that is needed to make the program more effective.

Program and Governance

At a minimum, the board of directors should approve new program initiatives. Ideally, board members should be among the first to ask the hard questions that are needed to determine whether staff has done its homework in regard to:

- establishing a true need for the program;
- determining the link between the program and the mission;

- researching existing models;
- collaborating where possible; and
- and working within the organization's capacity and ability to raise funds.

The board should require that an evaluation component exists to ensure that the program remains relevant and responsive to constituent needs into the future and is cost-effective and financially sound. The board may also want to review the broad program policies to ensure that the organization's values and ethics are reflected in the program's design. In very small organizations, the board's role may include implementing the program.

Collaboration

Community needs, particularly those addressed by social service and community-based agencies, have become so complex that no one agency can make a significant difference without strong linkages and collaboration with other nonprofits. In the past, government and private funders' insistence on collaboration has often met with great resistance from nonprofits – for good reason. Collaboration must come from the participants – not from those outside the system, no matter how well-intentioned the suggestion.

Smart organizations will collaborate; they know they can leverage their missions by working strategically with others. Truly collaborative organizations will partner at multiple levels – with constituents and community, with donors, and with other agencies whose values, vision, and interests are similar.

Why Collaborate?[1]

- Many sets of eyes and ears are needed to keep up with, interpret, and effectively move community-wide agendas forward.
- The pace of change – political, economic, social, and technological – is faster than ever before, calling for greater fluidity in service delivery and a greater range of strengths and skills.
- The ability to mobilize greater numbers of people and create critical mass increases the power to effect change.
- To be truly effective, we need the engagement of all those who care about the people and communities in which we work.

Selected Tips for Collaborators

- *Know thyself.* Make your own determination whether to collaborate and with whom to collaborate on the basis of the organization's mission, values, philosophy of service delivery, and constituent needs. *For example,* a consumer-led mental health advocacy group might find more alignment with a homeless-led organization than with a mental health organization of professionals.
- *Know your partners.* Find out how closely you share values and intentions and use this knowledge to guide the breadth and depth of activities on which you collaborate. Start with smaller-scale, shorter-term collaborations, and move to more depth and breadth as the collaboration matures.
- *Bring as much clarity to the collaboration as possible.* Discuss and reach agreement on expectations, structures, systems (especially communication systems), and plans for evaluation. Determine the following:
    - Who will be involved in the collaboration, association, or coalition?
    - What will be the membership requirements for agencies and individuals?
    - How will participation be ensured and developed among *all* members and not just a vocal minority?
    - Who will make decisions, and how will they be made?
    - Who will facilitate meetings?
    - Who will keep minutes and provide other administrative services?

[1]Taken from the Nonprofit Quarterly, "Community Building" edition, and from a workshop presented by Third Sector New England and sponsored by State Street Foundation.

- *Learn actively.* Use what works in practice to build stronger agreements and greater collaborative efforts.
- *Think systematically.* Be clear about your priorities and the kind of change you want to help create. Stay open to the perspectives and ideas of others who share your interests. Seek common ground toward developing a future all partners desire.
- *Evaluate your progress.* Assess your outcomes and periodically question your assumptions; continually talk and work together to improve them.
- *Be prepared to make mistakes.* Crossing boundaries of organization, rank, function, culture, class, and sector can lead to sticky situations. Openly acknowledge and work through the tough times so that all can learn what works and what doesn't. Challenge, but be patient with the honest mistakes of others.
- *Talk openly, but listen more than you talk.*
- *Honor your commitments to the collaboration.*

To Merge or Not to Merge?

Mergers are increasingly seen by funders as a way to contain administrative costs and free up program funding, especially among nonprofits providing similar services within a geographic region. Although these outcomes may be achieved in some cases, they are not automatic and should not be taken for granted. The costs of evaluating the feasibility of, and planning for, a merger can be extremely high – even if the merger does not happen. In addition, merging means the irreversible loss of a distinct organization. It is not something to be taken lightly.

Nonprofit organizations exist to fulfill a charitable purpose and are "owned" by the public and their constituents as represented by their boards of directors. Unlike business corporations, whose bottom line is profit, the "bottom line" for nonprofits is mission. The framing question for nonprofits, therefore, should be whether their *mission* would be better served by a merger. The potential for saving on administrative costs, while important, should be of secondary importance.

The question of merging, along with a serious, objective analysis of the pros and cons, should be put to the organization's key stakeholders in the form of surveys, focus groups, and one-on-one meetings. If possible, these activities should be led by an objective third party who can synthesize stakeholder feedback and provide it to the organization and its board of directors. The board is the ultimate decision maker.

A cautionary note: Funders often believe that one way to cure highly dysfunctional organizations is to merge them with healthier organizations. In such a scenario, however, the funder is shirking responsibility either to help out or to pull funding from the non-performing organization. Healthy organizations should be wary of adopting an agency with an unhealthy culture, no matter what assets, programs, or contracts it may bring.

Reasons to Merge

- The agency has outlived its primary purpose but has a few existing programs or assets that could be folded into another organization. Another option is for the board of directors to dissolve the agency and distribute its assets according to its bylaws.
- The client base has shrunk so significantly that fewer agencies are needed to respond to community need.
- Several agencies are duplicating services in a relatively small geographic area.
- An agency is at a critical juncture in its organizational development (or lack thereof), such as when a long-term leader is leaving or when a crisis in leadership has occurred. A merger may offer a better alternative than rebuilding all of the administrative infrastructure.
- The capacity for fundraising no longer exists and cannot be recaptured.
- The capacity for organizational health no longer exists and cannot be recaptured; however, such an organization should consider closing down

and transferring its assets to a similar nonprofit, or should commit to an intensive organizational intervention under the new parent organization.

Reasons Not to Merge

- A funder says so.
- It's the fad.
- They're doing it in the business world. Keep in mind that for-profit companies exist for different reasons and have a different bottom line. Fiscal expediency is important to well-run nonprofits, but cost-effectiveness must be weighed against the need for programming, the accessibility of services, etc.
- A larger, more aggressive agency wants to build an empire at the expense of a fine, smaller community-based organization.
- A tired board of directors thinks it is easier than reenergizing and reengaging the organization with its community and purpose.
- The agency is in financial trouble. If the community wants and needs the service, try other interventions first.

The Merger Process

Because the merger process tends to be all-consuming, make sure that the entire organization understands the need to investigate the possibility of a merger. Start by identifying several organizations that could be approached. Create a tool to screen for program compatibility, shared values, and organizational culture. Do not proceed if these basics do not match. Move on to another agency that will be closer to your values, culture, and philosophy of service delivery.

Understand that any decision about merger is likely to create anxiety among staff. You may not be able to relieve this anxiety entirely, but you can facilitate a process to surface it and thereby minimize its potential to create dysfunction.

A Checklist for Those Considering a Merger[2]

Once you have found an agency that shares your values and is willing to talk, this checklist can guide you through the process.

Preliminary Meetings and Discussion

- ☑ Identify a merger committee, and write job descriptions for the committee members.
- ☑ Identify a list of taskforces and subcommittees, and put each group's "charge" in writing.
- ☑ Develop a list of criteria for a merger, beginning with your vision and shared values and moving toward your business objectives.
- ☑ Develop a timetable for addressing each task and issue.
- ☑ Develop a draft budget for the merger process.
- ☑ Identify professional advisors.
- ☑ Plan for the early involvement of critical stakeholders and constituencies.

Preliminary Agreements

- ☑ Create a confidentiality agreement to protect information that is exchanged.
- ☑ Establish a memorandum of understanding that covers objectives, confidentiality, merger committee and task force assignments, a preliminary timetable for due diligence, and initial action items.

Structural/Organizational Issues

- ☑ Determine the form and structure of the new entity.
- ☑ Determine the process for selecting the new executive director.
- ☑ Determine the composition of the membership and the board of directors of the new entity.
- ☑ Agree upon the early involvement of, and communication with, staff and other stakeholders.

[2]This checklist is adapted from "Mergers, Acquisitions and Network Formation," a handout from the May 8, 1995 presentation by Brown, Rudnick, Freed & Gesmer at The Boston Foundation. Presented by Lawrence B. Litwak and Jeffrey Chase-Lubitz.

Operational, Program, and Staff Issues

- [x] Consolidate administrative functions and facilities.
- [x] Consolidate vendor agreements.
- [x] Consolidate fundraising plans.
- [x] Consolidate programs.
- [x] Consolidate staff. Plan for any changes in job descriptions, layoffs, and union negotiations, if necessary. Review and consolidate pension and fringe benefit programs.

When you reach this stage, it is time to hire an attorney, if you haven't already done so. The attorney can help create a checklist for due diligence, but this list should, at a minimum, cover consents; assignments; releases; existing contractual agreements held by either agency; third-party reimbursement analysis and impact; financial analysis; tax issues; regulatory issues; licensing; the legal mechanics of board votes; and the revision and filing of documents.

EVALUATION

CHAPTER 4

This chapter provides an overview of traditional evaluation basics, including types, methods, tools, and definitions. We start by reviewing types of standard evaluation to help readers gain an understanding of the field. Then we focus on simpler methodology, such as outcome measurement, which is the most commonly used method of evaluation for small and mid-sized nonprofits. We also look at feedback loops, which are part of the emerging trend for creating "smart" organizations where the staff continually learns through the use of ongoing feedback circles that link to cycles of continuous planning and program redesign. Our goal is to provide a more day-to-day, user-friendly way to evaluate programs.

Demystifying Evaluation

Program evaluation has become an academic field of research and investigation most often practiced by professional evaluators. The field of evaluation, which is actually a rather young social science, has developed a terminology that has become so scientifically and academically based that it is often difficult for non-practitioners to understand.

Scientific, academic style evaluation has its place and can be quite useful in some situations. But the cost, level of scientific rigor, and academic terminology has made evaluation frightening, off-putting, or simply boring to the majority of action-oriented, program-focused nonprofit managers and staff. And it has caused us to lose sight of the fact that *any ordinary person, including program participants, can engage in figuring out whether or not a program is effective,* a system is working, or an agency is having an impact. Done well, a simple, yet relevant, evaluation practice can significantly improve a program's effectiveness.

Why Evaluate?

Accountability is the primary reason for evaluation. Many small and mid-sized nonprofits conduct formal evaluations because it is required by their funders. Government agencies, foundations, United Way, and even individual donors are scrutinizing nonprofits more closely for accountability and effectiveness. Program participants, boards, staff, and the public are also demanding greater accountability. Nonprofit organizations are finding that it makes sense to place new emphasis on evaluation in order to:

- prove they are worthy of the public trust and the dollars given to them;
- show contributors that their social investment is working;
- ensure that the people for whom the organization exists are receiving tangible, real benefits;
- better understand staffing patterns and program delivery from a management perspective;
- plan; and
- do a better job.

Who Should Evaluate?

Almost anyone can evaluate. Participatory evaluation enables users of services to take part in designing and implementing the evaluation of those services. The style and values of the organization and the programs being evaluated will determine who participates in the evaluation process. A flatter, more inclusive organization is likely to include more people in the evaluation process. Different types of programs or activities will call for different types of evaluations and different levels of involvement.

Generally, the board of directors is accountable for ensuring that evaluation is taking place, whereas the executive director is responsible for managing the evaluation process. *Executive directors have the role of cultivating an atmosphere of openness, continuous learning, and skill at hearing constructive criticism at all levels of the organization.* An executive director must have these skills and competencies to successfully lead an organization that continually learns, innovates, and improves on behalf of its clients and its mission.

Leadership must demonstrate a spirit of belief in the importance of evaluation. If evaluation is dismissed by the executive director as an annoyance forced upon the agency from the outside, staff will feel the same way. The executive director must also understand the level of evaluation that is appropriate. It does not make sense to burden program staff with evaluation plans that are so time-consuming they don't have time to run the program. Be aware of how ready your organization is to create and implement new systems and structures.

It is not appropriate for the executive director to be the evaluator, but he or she needs to provide impetus, resources, and attention to evaluation. The task is to demonstrate a management commitment that speaks to the importance of evaluation by using evaluation itself to coach staff to new heights, involve clients in services, create better programs, increase publicity, and improve funding for the organization.

Organizational Transparency

Organizational transparency is the state an agency reaches when it can communicate clearly and openly about itself at all levels to all stakeholders, including the staff, board, clients, funders, and community constituents. Evaluation will help to create the clarity needed and lay a fact-based foundation for telling the organization's story. Anecdotal stories serve a purpose, but they do not "prove" the organization's relevance to the community with the same credibility that formal evaluation does.

Nonprofits are ultimately accountable to the public. As the information age demands more data and open communication, organizational transparency will continue to increase. Key stakeholders need to know that the organization is holding true to its mission through meaningful programs supported by sound management practices. Evaluation is the tool for demonstrating accountability.

Framing Questions for Evaluation, or What Do You Need to Consider?

It is important to be very clear about *what* you are evaluating, *why* you are evaluating, and *for whom* you are evaluating. Paying attention to these questions will help you shape your evaluation into a more useful tool.

What Are You Evaluating?

Think about what you are evaluating. Is it a start-up initiative? Ongoing services? Outcomes for program participants? The effectiveness of management functions such as internal communication, public relations, fund development, or governance? You will use different types of evaluation and different tools depending upon what you want to evaluate.

Why Are You Evaluating?

Why are you evaluating certain activities? Being clear about why and what you are evaluating will help you figure out how to evaluate it.

- Is it to find out if the activities are helping clients?
- To inform future planning?
- To understand better how an initiative got off the ground?
- To find out if activities are having an overall impact?
- To understand the impact of the activities on the organization?

Each of these questions gives rise to a different type of evaluation.

Who Is Your Target Audience?

How you package the findings of the evaluation will change depending upon the audience it is intended to reach. Is the evaluation:

- Internal to a team or department?
- For the staff of an organization?
- For the management team?
- For clients?
- For the entire agency?
- For the funders?
- For the general public?

Evaluation measures merit and value, *but it is also a communication tool,* one of the most effective a nonprofit can have.

Evaluation Basics

Types of Standard Evaluation[1]

Needs Assessment: A needs assessment is a way to explore the extent and depth of an issue or problem in such a way that a group can determine whether a case can be made for addressing the need. A needs assessment can determine the number and characteristics of individuals or institutions that would constitute the targets of a program. It can also be used to help design new programs or justify the continuation of existing programs.

Monitoring: Monitoring of activities produces regular, information that answers questions about whether a program or project is being implemented as planned. Monitoring helps identify problems and facilitate resolution in a timely way.

Formative Evaluation: Formative evaluation answers questions about how to improve and refine an ongoing program or a program that is being developed. Formative evaluation usually is undertaken during the initial or design phase of a project. It can, however, be helpful in assessing the activities of an established program. Formative evaluation puts data collection systems into effect early in the life of the program, capturing data that might not be available later on. Formative evaluation may include process and impact studies. Typically, the findings from a formative evaluation are provided as feedback to the program staff after an initial start-up period to help them make corrections during the course of the program's life.

For example:
A needs assessment has shown that a certain number of girls in high school have experienced dating violence. You decide to create a program to address this problem. Formative questions might include:

- What is the number of girls who can be served by this program?
- How many of those girls are being reached?
- Of those being reached, how many are choosing to participate in the program?
- Which approach for reaching girls is working and why?
- Can this approach be extended to reach more girls?

The answers to these questions can lead to program refinements that could increase the number of girls participating.

A *summative evaluation* might include similar questions, but it would take place at the end of the program, in order to judge the program's effectiveness retrospectively.

Outcome Evaluation: Outcome evaluation assesses the effectiveness of a program in producing change. Outcome evaluation focuses on difficult questions that ask what happened to program participants and how much of a difference the program made for them. Impact or outcome evaluation is useful when it is important to know whether and how well the objectives of a project or program were met.

For example:
Outcome questions for a smoking program might include:

- Did the program succeed in helping people to stop smoking?
- Was the program more successful with certain groups of people than with others?
- What aspects of the program did participants find gave the greatest benefit?

Process evaluation: Process evaluation documents the process of a program's implementation. Process evaluation helps stakeholders see *how* a program outcome or impact was achieved. The focus of a process evaluation is on the types and quantities of services delivered, the beneficiaries of those services, the resources used to deliver the services, the practical problems encountered, and the ways such problems were resolved.

For example:
Process evaluation questions might include:

- What specific interventions were put into place by the program in order to tackle the problem?
- How many communities were selected for pilot programs, and how were they selected?
- What were the kinds of problems encountered?
- How were the problems resolved?

[1]Much of this section is paraphrased or quoted from *Evaluation for Foundations,* a publication of the Council on Foundations, Jossey-Bass Publishers, San Francisco, 1993.

Information from process evaluation is useful for understanding how program impact and outcome were achieved and for program replication.

Participant-oriented Evaluation: Participant-oriented evaluation, although often described in a variety of ways, has several universal characteristics.

- Participant-oriented evaluation emphasizes the human element of an activity, focusing on describing and interpreting what is taking place in the program and the context in which it is taking place, rather than attempting to yield conclusive judgments.
- Participant-oriented evaluation is responsive to the flow of the program, rather than rigidly conforming to predetermined evaluation plans.
- Participant-oriented evaluation allows for differing values or viewpoints to be expressed, rather than holding that a particular value is the correct one.

Participant-oriented evaluation employs a variety of methods, including interviews, observation, and document review. It is especially useful in programs where it is important to capture feelings, reactions, and behavioral changes that cannot be easily quantified.

Proponents of participant-oriented evaluation believe that it has a greater potential than other evaluation approaches for learning about a program's effects because of its openness, flexibility, and sensitivity to human issues.

For example:
Participant-oriented evaluation is appropriate for programs designed to bolster self-esteem. Few standardized instruments, such as scales, surveys, and self-measures, could adequately assess changes in self-esteem after exposure to a program. A participant-oriented evaluator would observe the program in operation, review documents such as records from group meetings, and would note if participants showed changes that are difficult to quantify, such as having more hope for the future, seeking adequate housing, or, making life-changing decisions as a result of the program.

Selected Methods of Evaluation

Listed below are some of the most often used evaluation methods:

Quantitative evaluation methods: This method uses data collection and statistical methods to produce numerical values to describe the outcome of a program or project.

Qualitative evaluation method: This method is used to produce narrative descriptions of activities, processes, and outcomes that are generally based on observation and interviews.

Sampling: Sampling draws information from a *representative or random* portion of a total population to make judgments about the whole. Sampling is used with the survey technique or for select observations from a compilation of records.

Survey: A survey involves the preparation of a series of questions, specifically tailored to evaluate a program, which are then asked of program participants or other program stakeholders. A survey can be performed through face-to-face or telephone interviews, or self-administered questionnaires. It can be distributed randomly, to a representative sampling, or to all program participants, depending on the purpose of the survey.

About surveys: A survey should

- be as short as possible, written in simple, neutral language, and accompanied by clear directions;
- use closed-end (yes or no) questions as much as possible and guard against asking leading questions; and
- leave as little as possible to interpretation by the survey reader.

The survey tool must be valid for the evaluation itself to be valid. In developing a survey, it is important to seek help from books, classes, or experts in the community.

Testing: Testing measures an individual's acquired skills. It is most often used in learning-related programs. Pre- and post-testing can be used to more accurately gauge the learning that can be attributed to the program being evaluated. Questions on pre- and post-tests should be simple and close-ended, and should leave little to interpretation.

Observation: This method depends on using an objective third party to observe an activity. The observer can use quantitative methods of counting or categorizing behaviors or qualitative methods of observing activities and reporting on progress in a more general way.

Document analysis: This type of analysis involves the review and compilation of existing records and materials within files, such as intake and exit interviews, and other documents.

Anecdotal method: This method involves informal assessments by a group, such as program staff, that has begun to see or feel a trend that has not yet been documented. Anecdotal evidence is often used to determine when to do a needs assessment.

Outcome Measurement

Many funders, most notably United Way of America, have simplified evaluation requirements to avoid overwhelming grantees with evaluation projects that are beyond the scale of the programs being evaluated. This outcome measurement approach has two basic goals:

- To see if the program really makes a difference in the lives of people and
- To help organizations improve services.

The *outcome measurement approach* is an accessible evaluation approach, intended for use by people without a background in evaluation. Outcome measurement focuses on the benefits to the program participant. It is attractive to community-based nonprofits because it allows them to develop their own outcomes with input from agency stakeholders instead of having outcomes imposed on them by funders, regulatory bodies, or other groups outside the organization.

The outcome measurement process is a more participatory form of evaluation in that stakeholders, including consumers of services and other constituents, board members, staff, and community people can all be involved.

A Step-by-Step Outline of the United Way Model[2]

The outcome measurement approach[3] promoted by United Way of America includes the following main steps:

- Get ready.
- Choose outcomes.
- Specify indicators for the outcomes.
- Prepare to collect data on your indicators.

Other steps involve trying out the outcome measurement system, improving any problems, analyzing data, and deciding how to report findings.

1. Getting Ready

The executive director's first steps are to:

- Choose an outcome measurement work group. The group should be representative of various perspectives within the organization, from front-line workers to management staff.
- Ensure there is a common understanding of terms. Following is a brief glossary of useful terms.
    - *Inputs* are resources dedicated to the program and include money, staff and staff time, facilities, equipment, supplies, and volunteers and their time.
    - *Activities* are what the program does with its inputs to fulfill its mission. Activities are the strategies that the organization undertakes to provide its services in a meaningful way.
    - *Outputs* are the products of program activities. Outputs can be measured in terms of work accomplished, using factors such as number of clients reached, number of classes taught, or number of materials distributed.

[2] United Way of Massachusetts Bay can provide its affiliates and other nonprofit organizations with more comprehensive information on outcome measurement than appears in this chapter.

[3] The majority of the following section is taken from *Measuring Program Outcomes: A Practical Approach,* a publication of United Way of America, by Harry Hatry, Therese van Houten, Margaret C. Plantz and Martha Taylor Greenway.

- *Outcomes* are the benefits or changes achieved by individuals or populations during or as a result of participating in program activities. Outcomes relate to behavior, skills, knowledge, attitudes, values, condition, and status. Outcomes are changes in behavior, knowledge, thought, ability, or condition following a program.
- *Indicators* are the pieces of information that tell you how well a program is doing regarding an outcome. For example, if the outcome for attending prenatal classes is assumed to be a healthy baby, then the indicators will be factors that demonstrate that a baby is healthy. Birth weight is considered a standard measure of the health of a baby, so birth weight becomes one of several indicators for determining a healthy baby outcome for prenatal classes.

Once the outcomes measurement team understands the basic concepts and evaluation goals and has received the support of the executive director and board of directors, the team must then:

- decide which program to evaluate first;
- develop a timeline;
- develop ways to engage stakeholders in defining program outcomes;
- choose which indicators will be used;
- develop the data collection system to quantify the indicators;
- run a pilot evaluation and tweak it before going ahead with the full scale effort; and
- decide the format of reporting and disseminating information.

2. Choosing Outcomes

Choosing outcomes is the most participatory aspect of outcome measurement. Reach wide and ask for input from past and current program participants, constituents, program staff, and volunteers. Conduct focus groups. Talk to funders. Ask programs that deliver similar services what they feel outcomes might be; ask about both short-term and long-term outcomes.

It is very important to have fairly specific outcomes to measure. Long-term outcomes like saving the world (or even one individual) are too broad and far-reaching. Too many factors influence an individual's life for any one program to claim success for completely changing a person's life. For example, a smoking cessation class may have a long-term outcome of helping an individual quit smoking, but it can not reasonably claim to save that person's life. A case could be made, however, that the class decreased the individual's chances of getting lung cancer – as long as the capacity exists within the agency to gather that data.

3. Specifying Indicators

Since indicators represent information showing that an outcome is being met, indicators must be specific, observable, measurable characteristics or changes that will represent achievement of the outcome. They must also identify the statistic (number or percentage) that will summarize the program's performance on the outcome.

For example, for a smoking cessation class, the key outcome is that participants stop smoking. Indicators could include:

- the number and percentage of participants who report that they have quit smoking by the end of the course;
- the number and percentage of participants who have not relapsed six months after the program was completed; and
- the number and percentage of participants who have not relapsed one, two or five years after the program was completed.

Comparison of Major Data Collection Methods[4]

Characteristic	Data Collection Method: Review of Program Records	Self-Administered Questionnaire	Interview	Rating by Trained Observer
Cost	Low	Moderate	Moderate to high, depending on how it is administered	Depends on availability of low-cost observers
Amount of training required for data collectors	Some	None to some, depending on how it is distributed	Moderate to high, depending on survey complexity and collectors' previous experience	Moderate to high, depending on complexity and subtlety of observations
Completion time	Short, depending on amount of data needed	Moderate to long, depending on how it is distributed	Long	Short to moderate
Response rate	High, if records contain needed data	Depends on how it is distributed	Generally moderate to good	High

4. Choosing Data Collection Methods

Major sources for data by which to measure progress on indicators are existing records, interviews, or surveys of individuals, tests, or the use of trained outside observers.

Major data collection methods for use in outcome measurement include:

- review of program records from the organization or other agencies, such as schools, hospitals, referral agencies, courts, law enforcement agencies, or health departments;
- self-administered questionnaires or interviews that reach specific individuals such as program participants, relatives of program participants, staff at referring agencies, organization staff, or volunteers of the agency;
- rating by an observer trained to rate behaviors, facilities, or environments; and
- mechanical tests and measurements such as scales or blood tests.

[4]Taken from *Measuring Program Outcomes: A Practical Approach,* a publication of United Way of America, by Harry Hatry, Therese van Houten, Margaret C. Plantz and Martha Taylor Greenway.

Sample Outcome Measurement Framework: Southside Children's Agency[5]

In this example, we list potential outcomes along with one or more measurable indicators to help determine whether the outcome has been met. We also include data sources and collection methods that can provide the necessary information.

Once indicators have been identified and analyzed, one can further analyze program data to look for factors that may influence how successfully the outcomes have been met.

Program: Teen Mother Parenting Education

Outcome	Indicator(s)	Data Source	Data Collection Method
Teens are knowledgeable of prenatal nutrition and health guidelines	Number and percent of program participants able to identify food items that are good sources of major dietary requirements	Participants	Self-administered survey after second week in the program
Teens follow proper nutrition and health guidelines	Number and percent of participants who do not smoke	Participants Teachers	Self-report on daily checklist Observation reported on record weekly
	Number and percent of participants who eat at least four calcium servings and one of each other nutritional group each day	Participants	"Healthy Baby" checklist for recording daily food intake
	Number and percent of participants within proper ranges for prenatal weight gain	School scales	Weekly weigh-ins
	Number and percent of participants who take a prenatal vitamin	Participants	"Healthy Baby" checklist for recording daily food intake
Teens deliver healthy babies	Number and percent of newborns weighing 5.5 pounds or above or scoring 7 or above on Apgar scale	Hospital records	Contact hospital for birth records

Influencing Factor	Data Source	Data Collection Method
Mother's age	Program records	Record review
Mother's household income	Program records (based on mother's self-report)	Record review
Number of parenting classes mother attended	Program records	Record review

5. Putting It All Together

The United Way model recommends that outcome measurement teams pretest their data collection instruments and procedures and conduct a pilot test of their measurement systems that includes analysis and reporting of their findings. They also recommend using the findings *internally* to change programs, support annual planning, and justify resource allocations, and *externally* to increase funding and/or enhance the agency's public image.

The bottom line of outcome measurement, however, is finding out if your program is having any real benefit for participants. It is the most "real" and useful evaluation method, particularly for human

[5]Taken from *Measuring Program Outcomes: A Practical Approach,* a publication of United Way of America, by Harry Hatry, Therese van Houten, Margaret C. Plantz and Martha Taylor Greenway.

service agencies, to come along and should prove instrumental in pushing the nonprofit sector toward better programs with improved outcomes for their constituents.

Emerging Trends – Feedback Loops

Organizations typically do well at setting goals and objectives for programs. They often fall short, however, when it comes to framing:

- *process* questions about how the program is being implemented;
- *formative* questions about how to improve the program mid-course; and
- *outcome/impact* questions about how to measure how well the program did on behalf of its clients.

Some organizations jump into projects without ever justifying the need through a *needs assessment,* simply because a leader thought it was a good idea.

Without solid information about the current environment and how well existing programs are doing, it is difficult to identify the next set of priorities and goals effectively.

Ongoing evaluation is a key part of providing information about current reality so that organizations can envision the future.

Smart organizations will begin to implement feedback cycles for individual programs that can facilitate change and innovation more quickly than formal evaluation allows. The same checklist that is used in Chapter 5, **Strategic Planning and Thinking,** to measure an organization's ability to think strategically, can be used to measure whether the organization is using meaningful feedback.

Strategically link planning and evaluation; the two activities are symbiotic. Ask the following questions, from the strategic planning checklist, that relate to evaluation:

- ☑ Does the organization *continuously gather data* from and about its external environment?
- ☑ Does the organization *learn from the past* and establish open, evolving plans focused on immediate issues?
- ☑ Does the organization *set intermediate goals that are measurable and observable*
- ☑ has the organization designated responsible individuals or teams for implementation?
- ☑ Does the organization encourage experimentation (from grassroots up), *measure improvement,* recognize, and reward and institutionalize positive change?
- ☑ Does the organization *support deep reflection* in the form of ongoing opportunities for reflection, questioning of underlying assumptions, and searching for deep systematic solutions/interventions to current problems?
- ☑ Does the organization *define its learning, planning, and evaluation cycle?*

A feedback loop can be as simple as the one described in the following diagram:

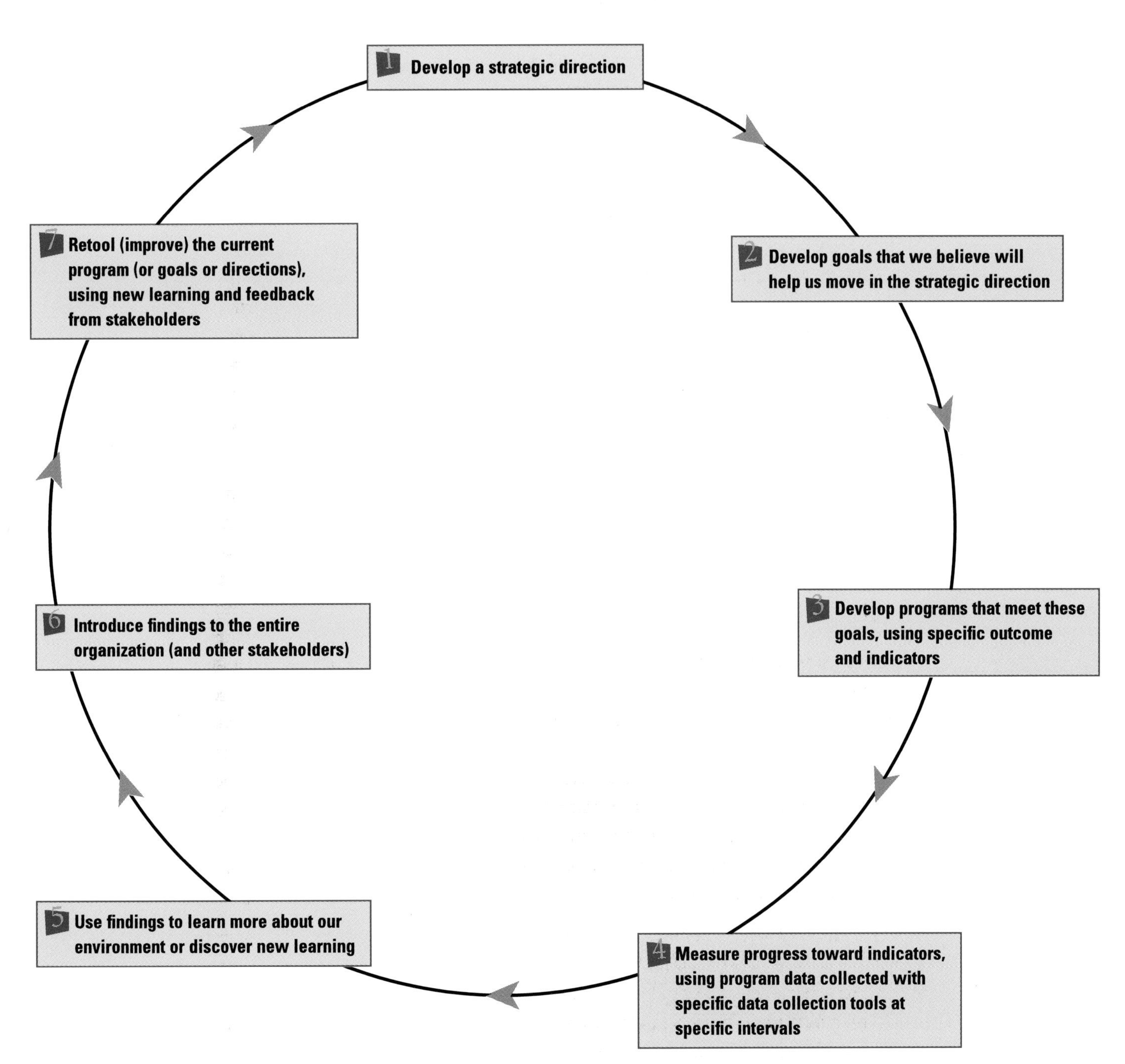

STRATEGIC PLANNING AND THINKING

CHAPTER 5

Strategic Planning and Thinking

Probably no other function is changing as much as the way organizations plan. The nonprofit environment is changing so quickly that three-year plans are generally hopelessly out-of-date after one or two years. As a result, many groups are beginning to do quick-cycle adapting and retooling – what we call *strategic thinking*. Strategic *planning* still has merit, however, especially as it emphasizes revisiting the organization's mission, vision, and values. In this chapter, we discuss the basics of strategic planning and offer some suggestions for moving an organization toward strategic thinking.

Why Plan?

Planning gives stakeholders a road map for the near future. Planning also strengthens an organization's capacity to adopt relevant programming, evaluate operations, and change as the environment demands. Rapidly changing environments demand smart organizations with committed, well-trained people focused on mission, values, and continuous personal growth. Such people will govern, work, and volunteer best in environments where the values, workplace expectations, strategies, and goals have been articulated clearly and are understood widely.

The best planning is dynamic and can be changed mid-course, rather than static, with rigid goals that people check off as they are accomplished. *Strategic* planning provides a guide for reaching sometimes lofty destinations.

Strategic planning:

- *creates* guidelines for the future;
- *opens* ongoing dialogue regarding best practices and programming for fulfilling the mission of the organization;
- *engages* a broad spectrum of people in assuming ownership of the organization;
- *forms* the true foundation of a good fundraising plan, giving development staff real strategies and activities (not just programs) to market to donors;
- *builds* a solid foundation for program and staff evaluations by articulating clear goals that create a baseline from which to judge performance;
- *develops* skills in the staff who participate; and
- *enables* clear articulation of values, which is particularly important when building internal work teams or deciding to enter into collaboration with other organizations where shared values are crucial to success.

Strategic planning should *not* be used if:

- The organization is in crisis. Address the crisis first. Don't use strategic planning to avoid dealing with communication, leadership, or financial management problems.
- Resources are inadequate. When time, people, or financial resources are in short supply, create a short-term plan to build them. All these resources need to be in place for the organization to plan well.
- Intuition works well among the leaders of the organization. Take advantage of leaders who instinctively (and accurately) assess the organization's strengths and weaknesses, internal and external influences, place within the community, natural collaborators and true competitors. Give freedom to leaders who naturally focus all of the agency's resources on future goals, strategically linking support functions like fund development and human resources to the organization's vision of the future. Help intuitive planners design ways to include others in the planning that they do so naturally in order to build capacity within others to think as strategically as they do.

Definitions of Some Common Terms Used in Strategic Planning

Mission describes the purpose of the organization – the reason it exists.

Strategic thinking is the process of continuous planning that enables staff, clients, and other stakeholders to add their voices and input to the decision-making process. Strategic thinking emphasizes continuous learning and feedback cycles at the level where most of the work is done. It allows for changes in direction, goals, and activities (while staying within the mission) as needed in response to the fast-paced environment we live in.

Preferred future vision paints a picture of the future the organization is seeking to create. It gives shape and direction to the organization's future.

Strategic direction is the overall direction – the strategies and priorities – that help guide the organization toward its preferred future.

Values[1] are our beliefs in action. They guide our behavior as we take action on a day-to-day basis to realize our vision and purpose. Our set of values might include:

- how we want to behave with each other;
- how we regard our customers, community, and vendors; and
- which lines we will and will not cross.

Values are best expressed in terms of behavior. If we act as we should, what would an observer see us doing? When values are made a central part of the organization, they become a guide for behavior that will help people move toward the shared vision with honesty and transparency.

Goals are the specific milestones that the organization plans to reach in the not-too-distant future. Goals can be used in evaluation to help determine organizational effectiveness.

Key actions are the more important or larger activities or steps that move agencies toward meeting goals. Actions should be concrete and time-specific.

Outcomes are measurable early-, mid-, or long-term program results that agencies want to reach on behalf of program participants.

Traditional Steps in Strategic Planning

- Plan to plan. Identify who the stakeholders will be in the process and set a timeline.
- Assess the current situation. Review the relevance of the mission and programs. Describe the recent "story" of the organization to create an historical context.
- Make an honest assessment of the organization's strengths and weaknesses.
- Look at the economic, political, and demographic environments that influence the agency. Consider potential collaborations and competitors.
- Work with stakeholders to define the broad strategic directions of the organization.
- Design a way to check in on the plan and evaluate progress against stated goals and activities.
- Make the plan operational by attaching time lines, assigning responsibilities to people, and creating a budget.
- Implement.

Organizations accomplish these steps in different ways. Those with intuitive planners at the helm may take them informally, but continuously. Most organizations create an *ad hoc* strategic planning committee. Some create committees which include board members only; some include board members and staff; still others will invite stakeholders, including clients, community members, and funders to participate on the committee.

These *ad hoc* committees are usually responsible for laying out the steps and determining a time line for developing the plan. Many organizations find it useful to engage a consultant to help with the process.

Allow at least six months for a full-fledged strategic planning process. For the average busy, mid-sized nonprofit, it will take some time to:

- gather internal and external data;
- hold retreats with board and staff to look at mission, purpose, and future vision;
- recommit or change organizational values;
- hold meetings or retreats to establish strategies, goals, and key actions; and
- develop consensus.

(See **Comparing the Differences Between Strategic Planning and Strategic Thinking** and **A Checklist for Thinking Strategically** later in this chapter.)

[1] Senge, Peter. *The Fifth Discipline: the Art and Practice of the Learning Organization.* New York: Doubleday/Currency, 1990.

Case Study: Elizabeth Stone House

The Elizabeth Stone House was founded in 1974 by former mental health patients as an alternative therapeutic program for women in emotional distress and their children. The organization has usually been years ahead of the mainstream on issues such as the relationship between violence and its effect on a woman's mental health. It was one of the first programs in the country to develop transitional housing and to focus on women's economic development as a distinct need. Although the Stone House had often been in the vanguard of such programming, it has rarely developed a formal strategic plan.

The organization credits its vision to several aspects of its organizational structure, which is fairly flat, and its philosophy of service delivery, which remains client-centered and mission-focused. It uses its mission as a screen in nearly all functions–decision making, planning, fund development and human resources.

The organization's hiring process uses scenario-style questions to determine the prospective employee's match to mission and organizational values–as well as with skills needed.

New hires are put through rigorous training. New hires spend the first six months learning a position or "area of expertise." The second six months emphasize learning and skill development around making informed, management-level decisions within a team structure. Stone House relies completely on the concept of teams, even at the level of "executive director." Actually, there is no director. Rather, a team of staff who have learned enough over time become part of a group that makes executive management decisions.

All staff are required to understand the root causes of the issues that bring women and children to their doors, including: mental illness, domestic violence, and poverty. Continual reflection on these root causes is promoted and a shared analysis is developed and changed as needed. Individual staff members and teams are also required to develop annual action plans based on an analysis of program successes or failures of the previous year. The flatter organizational structure, deep emphasis on mission and values, purposeful hiring and orientation of new staff, and insistence upon individual, team and organizational capacity to think critically of the root causes of social problems benefits individual staff members and constituents as well as program development. Because the organization rewards critical thinking and values innovation, short-term action planning can grow into larger scale projects, such as the organization's development of the first transitional housing projects in the country.

In order to create an organization that thinks as strategically as Stone House does, consider the following: (1) Strengthen your mission and values focus and make it widespread throughout your organization; (2) Develop a shared analysis of the critical issues your organization exists to address; (3) Develop structures that foster dialogue, critical thinking and decision making on the front lines, where the staff are closest to clients and their issues; and (4) Develop structures for honest feedback on "How are we really doing?" and ongoing action planning that evolves naturally into larger projects and more comprehensive responses as the need emerges.

Developing People Who Think Strategically

Developing an organization of people who think strategically is different from developing an organization that knows how to plan strategically. Strategic thinking differs from strategic planning in that it:

- is not a static process taken on every three or five years.
- involves planning and evaluation activities that include feedback loops and greater participation than the typical linear, hierarchical planning process.

- is deeply rooted in the fabric of the organization and is most actively undertaken at the front lines.
- depends on the strength of the organization's human resources or "people practices." Front-line staff need to be given the tools to develop the skills to become strategic thinkers. Staff development is the key indicator of capacity, or "readiness," whereas in traditional strategic planning, indicators for readiness are the commitment and willingness to plan by key decision makers at the executive director or board level.
- creates a plan from the ground up, based on observed and documented needs of the community or constituency.
- involves an identifiable learning cycle that overlaps human resource functions such as developing team and individual work plans, supervision and evaluation, but also involves cycles of learning, planning, evaluating, learning again, planning, and evaluating.

The learning cycle makes room for conversations that:

- *question* the plan while it is still in process so that it can be refined and modified through insights that have been gained from the implementation efforts;
- *reflect* on what has been learned through implementation and evaluation;
- *revise* vision, strategies, and action plans whenever necessary, not just during a formal planning process; and
- *encourage* improvisation.

An organization that emphasizes strategic thinking recognizes that learning is different for each person. To develop your organization's strategic thinking, provide coaching for staff to help them see beyond individual roles and understand the whole system of the organization and its field of work. Allow teams and individuals to think creatively and "push the envelope" in exploring new ways to work toward meeting priorities. If possible, increase the organization's budget to allow for modest experiments and/or grassroots innovations, and then promote the most successful efforts throughout the whole system.

A Checklist[2] for Thinking Strategically

Use this checklist to see if your organization is thinking strategically or is on its way to doing so.

- ☑ Does the organization create strategy continuously from a shared vision and map of current reality?
- ☑ Does the organization gather data continuously from and about its external environment?
- ☑ Does the organization learn from the past? Has it established open, revolving plans focused on immediate issues?
- ☑ Does the organization set intermediate goals that are measurable and observable? Have individuals or teams been designated to be responsible for implementation?
- ☑ Does the organization encourage experimentation (from grassroots up); measure improvement; and recognize, reward, and institutionalize positive change?
- ☑ Does the organization support deep reflection in the form of ongoing opportunities for contemplation, questioning of underlying assumptions, and searching for deep systematic solutions and interventions for current problems?

[2]Checklist developed by Dakota Butterfield, who was one of the consultants to the COMMONGROUND project that brought 17 Boston area community-based organizations together to explore collaborative management practices over a three year period.

Comparing the Differences between Strategic Planning and Strategic Thinking

Strategic Planning

Planning to Plan

1. The board approves the process periodically, such as in three- to five-year intervals.
2. The process is triggered by the completion of a previous plan or by a crisis in the organization.
3. Planning is led by the board of directors and the executive director.
4. Roles are fairly defined: leader, follower, data gatherer, assessment team, priority identifiers, goal setters, and implementers.
5. Planning and evaluation assumptions must be clear.
6. There is a set timetable and work plan.
7. Stakeholders are identified.

Assessing the situation

1. There is a large, planned effort to assess the environment, and to identify external opportunities and threats as well as internal strengths and weaknesses.
2. The process includes summarizing critical issues for the future.

Strategic Thinking

Planning to Plan

1. The board policy is to create an organization that thinks strategically.
2. The process is ongoing and deeply rooted and is capable of adapting in crises.
3. Planning is led by front-line staff and constituents.
4. Roles are fluid with people taking on responsibility according to their skills, expertise, and level of impact on their work and lives.
5. Planning and evaluation assumptions must be clear.
6. Work is ongoing, and the timetable is fluid and defined by the learning cycle – how quickly the group learns from an experiment, challenge, or crisis.
7. Stakeholders are identified, but participation is constantly revisited through evaluation and an inclusion lens.

Assessing the situation

1. Small evaluation/assessment projects are attached to every project and identify critical questions, such as:
   - Are we meeting true constituent or community needs?
   - Is our process working?
   - Are outcomes valuable to those we are serving?
   - Is it cost-effective and manageable?
2. The process includes summarizing critical issues for the future but often in different venues with the board, consumers, staff, and community. Critical issues can also be identified by what a group perceives or "feels" are emerging trends.

Strategic Planning	Strategic Thinking
3. Mission and visions statements are updated periodically.	3. Mission, vision, and values are used as screens for major decisions and are an integral part of programming. All work, including hiring, orientation, training, supervision, and evaluation is measured against these screens. Staff are "trained" to integrate the mission into all they do and to evaluate activities in the context of mission and vision.
Developing Activities	**Developing Activities**
1. The group develops strategies for meeting identified priorities that usually have been determined at a retreat with the board and staff.	1. The staff or a core group of coworkers determine how to involve consumers, constituents, the board and community members – people who can define priorities from various perspectives. Stakeholders may also include competitors, collaborators, and providers of resources.
2. Strategies are seen as answers and straight paths to the mission.	2. It is OK for strategies to raise more questions than they answer because the work of developing them will be a process of discovery. Hitting some dead ends along the way is not perceived as failure.
3. Goals and objectives for programs and management issues are usually defined by executives and managers.	3. End users, board members, and others are included in goal-setting. Decisions on how to measure the success of goals and objectives are made as part of this process, not at the end of the strategic planning process.
4. Action plans are developed by the staff.	4. Action plans are developed by the staff, but the action plans are informed by outcomes (what you will measure) as much as by goals (what you hope to achieve).
Drafting a Strategic Plan	**Drafting a Strategic Plan**
1. A plan is drafted and then revised with input from the organization.	1. Plans are written, revised, and/or discarded as needed. Mid-course corrections are the norm.
2. A defined mechanism exists for revising and changing the strategic plan.	2. The process for modifying the plan is fluid and ongoing.

Tools[3] for Continuous Planning (Strategic Thinking)

- Widely understood strategic priorities; written mission and vision statements.
- An accountability system that reinforces stewardship and staff development so that each individual gains the capacity to understand the underlying assumptions that may block him or her from working within a group to achieve an organizational vision.
- Continuous skill-building in communication, understanding larger organizational systems, awareness of the greater community, understanding the environmental context of an issue, including its history, current social trends and political impacts, and ability to learn, plan, and evaluate.
- A defined learning, planning, and evaluation cycle. The cycle can be as simple as the feedback loop described in Chapter 4, **Evaluation**, which includes the following steps:
    1. Have a strategic direction.
    2. Develop goals that support progress in the strategic direction.
    3. Develop programs that meet these goals, using specific outcomes and indicators.
    4. Measure progress toward indicators using program data collected with specific data collection tools at specific intervals.
    5. Use findings to learn about the organization's environment or to identify new learning needs.
    6. Introduce findings to the entire organization (and other stakeholders).
    7. Retool (improve) the current program (or goals or directions) as a result of new learning and feedback from stakeholders.

Tips for Planning (Strategic Thinking) in Nonprofit Settings

- Develop and institute ongoing staff training that enables staff to quickly "take ownership" and become stewards of mission, vision, values, and overall direction. (See Chapter 10, **Human Resources**.)
- Develop and institute educational programs for consumers, the board of directors, volunteers, constituents, collaborators, funders, community leaders, and the public. (See Chapter 8, **Public Relations**.)
- Coach staff to learn from the past. Provide training on the use of formal *and informal* evaluation techniques.
- Coach staff to anticipate multiple possible futures. Provide training in scenario planning, including the ability to re-vision quickly to address a crisis.
- Coach staff to focus on immediate business and concrete issues. Set ambitious short-term milestones and plan for quick learning by designing ways to "cycle" the immediate business through evaluation/reflection/learning/planning feedback loops. (See Chapter 4, **Evaluation**.)
- Coach staff to understand indicators of success. Provide training to help staff learn to identify, ask, and answer critical questions about the process for development and implementation of program activities.

[3]This piece was drawn from a discussion with Dakota Butterfield, colleagues in the COMMONGROUND project, and the work of Peter Senge in *The Fifth Discipline*.

GOVERNANCE

CHAPTER 6

The relationship between the executive director and the board of directors can set the tone for the entire organization. This storied partnership – or lack thereof – keeps many an organizational development consultant working long and hard. While the majority of nonprofit organizations have fine working boards, too many are characterized by power struggles, lack of open communication, inability to confront in a constructive manner, lack of shared vision and direction, tendencies to micromanagement, or lack of commitment – all of which lead to organizational dysfunction and constant turnover of executive directors. ***It need not be so.***

If you take nothing else from this chapter, at least consider this: *If all nonprofit boards focused on the mission, did not allow individual agendas and personalities to overwhelm the collective needs of the organization, and worked in partnership to define the organization's future, a great deal of dysfunction would disappear from the nonprofit sector.*

In this chapter, we will provide a grounding in good practice basics for traditional governance, an analysis of what sometimes goes wrong with traditional governance and the board/executive director relationship, some solutions for these problems, and an overview of emerging trends and characteristics of good governance.

Why Do Boards of Directors Exist?

Boards exist to help ensure that organizations uphold the "public trust" in their charitable purpose and remain worthy of the significant tax benefits that the government grants to charitable organizations under the Internal Revenue Service (IRS) tax code, section 501(c)(3). Nonprofit organizations are given these tax benefits because the IRS (for the government) has determined that their mission and activities benefit the common good. State and federal laws make boards of directors legally responsible for providing the oversight necessary to ensure that the charitable purpose is being served and that ethical standards are being upheld. Every 501(c)(3) eligible organization is required by law to be governed by a board of directors which acts on behalf of the general public, does not stand to gain financially from the charitable activities of the organization, and exists to provide prudent oversight of the overall operations and direction of the organization.

What Is Good Governance Anyway?

According to the authors of the *Harvard Business Review* article "The New Work of the Nonprofit Board":[1]

> "Effective governance by the board of a nonprofit organization is a rare and unnatural act. Only the most uncommon of nonprofit boards functions as it should by harnessing the collective efforts of accomplished individuals to advance the institution's mission and long-term welfare."

We believe effective governance *need not be so rare.* Executive directors and board members can work to focus the collective minds of the board on the mission, program effectiveness, and the long-term health of the organization. When it comes to governance, *less is generally better.* By "keeping it simple" and continually reinforcing the mission and vision of the organization, boards can stay focused on policy, oversight, and the setting of parameters within which management can move the organization forward. "Keeping it simple," however, *does not mean* relinquishing oversight responsibilities, failing to show up for meetings, or rubber-stamping a powerful executive director or board president.

Keeping it simple for good governance relies upon:

- the collective action of prudent people making well-informed decisions;
- a partnership among the board and the community, clients, management, and frontline staff to fulfill the mission;
- people at all levels of the organization who can clearly define and uphold the mission; and
- people who can set aside their individual egos and personal agendas for the collective good and benefit of the public the organization exists to serve.

[1] Barbara E. Taylor, Richard Chait, and Thomas P. Holland, "The New Work of the Nonprofit Board," *Harvard Business Review,* September-October 1996.

How Does Governance Work?

The board of directors is the entity that is legally responsible for the conduct and performance of the nonprofit organization. Traditionally, this legal responsibility has been viewed as having three fundamental legal duties which have been stated as:

- Duty of Care, which means acting in good faith consistent with what the board or individual board member truly believes is in the best interest of the organization;
- Duty of Loyalty, which means doing what is in the best interest of the organization; and
- Duty of Obedience, which means honoring and acting consistently with the requirements of applicable laws and the organization's mission, bylaws, policies, and other standards of appropriate behavior.

Fundamentally, board members must honor these standards of behavior in all decisions and actions related to the organization. Their governance responsibilities include:

- *defining and upholding* the mission and purpose of the organization;
- *designating* broad parameters and policies within which staff can manage, function, and experiment (defining ends, not means);[2]
- *ensuring* financial viability, which falls into two broad categories: (1) providing financial oversight through a treasurer or finance committee, and (2) planning for future viability through resource development;
- *maintaining* accountability to the client, staff, funders, community, and public, including a duty to evaluate effectiveness and incorporate feedback circles with various stakeholders;
- *ensuring* a healthy management function, which means providing for a qualified, skilled, and accountable executive director or, in alternatively structured organizations that operate without an executive director, ensuring that a strong and accountable management function exists; and
- *protecting* the strength and continuity of the board through succession planning and board development activities.

Boards typically meet their responsibilities by self-organizing into structures and systems that allow them to function and communicate. Traditionally, boards have allowed function to follow structure. We believe *boards should feel free to allow structure to follow function* and suggest: (1) limiting the number of standing committees that hold regular meetings, whether they have issues to discuss or not, and (2) encouraging the use of task forces and ad hoc committees that convene to meet strategic needs and disband when their issues have been dealt with. That said, keep in mind that the overall purpose of breaking the full board into committees is to *allow board meetings to focus on larger discussions* while the more detailed work is done in committees.

When boards design committee structures to ensure proper function, they generally create committees that parallel administrative functions within the agency – such as planning, program, fundraising, public relations, personnel, executive, and board development committees[3].

Governance Basics

Bylaws

Bylaws spell out how a corporation and its board will function. State law requires nonprofit organizations to have bylaws to become incorporated. Bylaws should generally be kept as simple and open-ended as possible to avoid endless amendments in the future. Basic bylaws should contain the following specifics about the board:

- the range in the number of members who will sit on the board;
- the length and number of terms of board members;
- the titles and roles of board officers;
- what constitutes a quorum for doing business, the frequency of board meetings, and other voting procedures; and

[2] John Carver has written extensively on "policy governance" by which the board sets the parameters within which management can achieve the "ends" set by the board.

[3] For more information on committee structure, we suggest contacting the National Council on Nonprofit Boards at 1-800-883-6262 or www.ncnb.org.

- other board procedures and responsibilities, such as resignations, removal from office, filling of vacancies, etc.

Terms of Office

Consider limiting the number of terms of office a board member can serve. Many organizations have found that allowing board members to serve for a maximum of six years gives them the year or two it takes to develop a deep understanding of the agency's mission and programs as well as a significant amount of time to contribute to meaningful and appropriate leadership. After six years, however, board members tend to become entrenched. Keep in mind that good board members can always find other ways to stay involved and can be invited back on the board after their break from the governance role. When term limits are in place, it is especially important to balance senior, knowledgeable board members with newer members.

Board Size: What Is the Right Size?

There is no right or wrong size, but recent trends show that large boards (over 30 members) appear to be falling out of favor. Such large boards tend to be run by executive committees that become cliques, with power concentrated in the hands of a few. The boards of small and mid-size nonprofits tend to range from 11 to 25 people. Boards should be large enough to provide the oversight that the IRS and the attorney general's office is seeking, but not so small that they become cozy clubs nor so large that they become social clubs where the true charge of governance is lost.

Incorporation

Each state has its own laws and regulations concerning how a nonprofit organization can become incorporated. In general, the secretary of state's office can provide specific information and any necessary forms.[4]

Tax-Exempt Status

Federal tax-exempt status is determined by the Internal Revenue Service. The IRS application process requires you to submit copies of the agency's bylaws, mission statement, and Articles of Incorporation.[5]

Full Board Responsibilities

The board as a whole is accountable for governance of the nonprofit organization. The full board should meet often enough to fulfill its legal obligation to provide oversight of the organization. While there are no absolute right or wrong numbers of meetings, meeting fewer than four times a year may be problematic. Many boards meet monthly or bimonthly.

Board meetings should be conducted with a written agenda (with length of time proposed for each item included on the agenda) that has been sent to board members ahead of time. It is common for the executive director and board president to prepare the agenda, with one of the two taking responsibility for sending it out. Unless there are compelling reasons, the board meeting should not be scheduled to last longer than two hours.

The board should have simple, straightforward bylaws that define its size, terms of its members, and voting procedures. Every board member should sign a conflict of interest statement. If the work of officers is complex, the board may want to consider creating written job descriptions for board officers; many organizations are developing written job descriptions for *all* board members. (See the Appendix for a sample conflict-of-interest statement and generic board job description.)

The full board should focus its attention on "bigger" issues, such as positioning the organization to flourish in changing times; long-range visioning; and developing broad policies. While many boards traditionally have devoted their meetings around hearing committee reports, a better system might be to organize meetings around the agency's top priorities for the year.

[4] In the Commonwealth of Massachusetts, application forms are available at and inquiries should be made to: Secretary of State, Corporate Division, Commonwealth of Massachusetts, One Ashburton Place, Boston, MA 02108. This office can be reached by telephone at 617-727-9640 or on the Internet at www.state.ma.us/sec.

[5] Start the process by requesting IRS Form 1023 and Publication 557 entitled "Tax Exempt Status for Your Organization." Copies are available on the IRS website www.irs.gov under Forms and Publications or by calling 800-829-1040.

Traditionally, the full board charges its committees to do the "legwork" for the board. One method for being clear about the "charge" of the committees is to create job descriptions not only for the committees, but also for the committee chairs – to help define the tasks needed to manage effectively, reach goals, and evaluate committee performance.

Committees can include non-board members as long as the non-board members are aware of the responsibilities and commitment that is required. Including others on committees is a good way to recruit and get to know volunteers who later may become board members. (See **Creating Boards of the Future** later in this chapter.)

Board as Boss or Board as Partner?

Many organizations are struggling with the old "command and control" model of governance (and management) and finding that it does not work well for nonprofit organizations. It is not flexible enough to help organizations meet their mission effectively, nor is it a good model for organizations working to

Governance Models

A Traditional Hierarchical Model

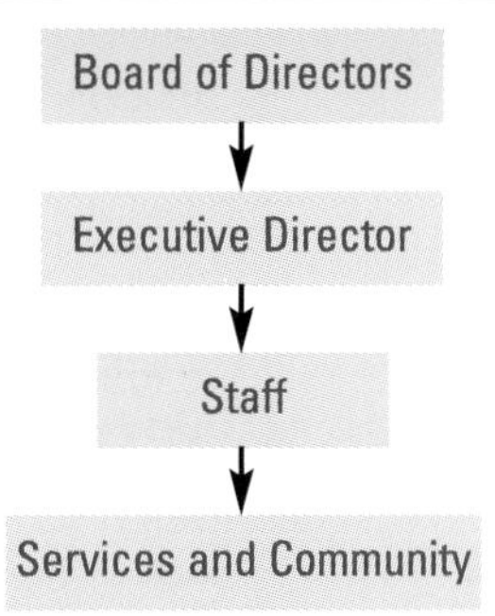

A Partnership Model of a Mission-Focused Nonprofit

The board governs with accountability to clients, community, and staff

The board and the executive director ensure that the organization is accountable to the broader community through open communication and feedback loops.

The executive director facilitates cross-function communication, partnership, and accountability

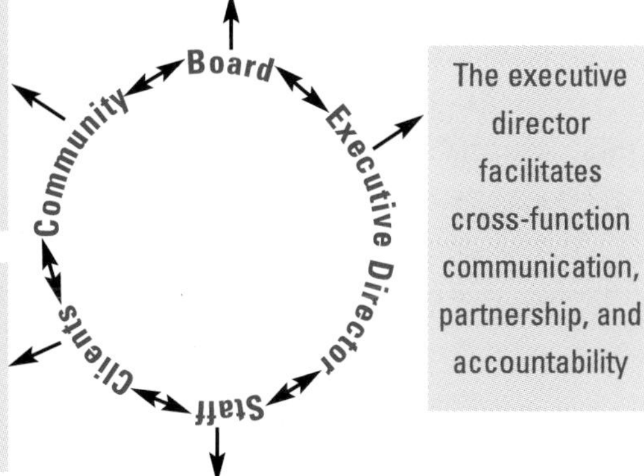

Clients inform new programs through feedback, formal evaluation, and participation in planning.

The staff implements programs, is empowered to make decisions as those closet to the work, and partners with clients.

empower people within and outside the organization. The hierarchical formula that seemed to work in the quickly fading industrial age does not help organizations navigate in the new information age. Today's environment requires staff and management who can respond quickly to changes in technology, consumer needs, and the economy, as well as to the increased demand for accountability by funders, constituents, consumers, and the general public.

Our preferred model of governance emphasizes partnership between the board and the agency's various stakeholders. In the partnership model, board members view themselves as partners with a set of stakeholders who also have ownership in, and accountability to, the organization. Management systems tend to be flatter or more circular under a partnership model, where it is clear that all stakeholders share in the responsibility of communicating with each other in managing the organization effectively.

Trends in Governing through Flexible Partnerships

Organizations often start as small, entrepreneurial endeavors that grow, adding staff, systems, facilities, and new programs. Naturally, the leadership style and level of governance will need to change as well, to fit the organization at any given stage of its life cycle. Unfortunately, most governance models are static, proposing similar governance structures and systems for all nonprofit organizations, regardless of their size, age, needs, or philosophy.

The executive director, in partnership with the board of directors, needs to understand where an organization is in its life cycle and to be honest about the leadership skills and attributes that are required to provide shared and appropriate levels of leadership at each juncture of the life cycle.

A core competency that should be required of those in governance and management is the ability to step back and honestly communicate the types of leadership roles, responsibilities, and partnerships that are important for a given period of time in an organization's life cycle. Sometimes a board will "follow" a strong staff. Sometimes it will lead the organization. Ideally, it will demonstrate flexibility in continually redefining its partnership with management and constituents in order to best serve the changing needs of the organization.

Our fast-changing environment will demand quick-cycle workplaces that can learn and adapt as needed. These "learning organizations" will be led best by those who understand the situational leadership and flexible partnering that is needed to meet the agency's mission in the twenty-first century's context of constant change.

Creating Flexible Partnerships

The relationship between the executive director and the board of directors will fit one of three basic styles: leading, following, or partnering. Much of the relationship will be defined by where the nonprofit is in its life cycle and the organization's recent history.

Executive directors and boards of directors are often too close to the organization to see clearly the impact organizational growth and life cycles have on relationships within the organization. Few people truly understand that different phases in the life of an organization call for different types of leadership – in both governance and management. This lack of understanding leads to repeatedly hiring executive directors who are the "wrong person at the wrong time," as well as to filling the board with people with appropriate skills, but not the right amount of "team-ness." (See Chapter 13, **Managing Change**, for an explanation of organizational life cycles and the leadership styles required most during those cycles.)

Most people do not join a nonprofit organization – either as board member or as executive director – with the intention of creating dysfunction. And yet, far too much dysfunction is allowed to exist within our organizations, particularly at the governance and management level, because the people involved do not have the perspective and tools to root it out.

When people problems divert attention from the mission, hard times result. Each difficult experience creates its own little pool of disappointment, distrust, and dysfunction. Others within the organization get caught up in the pieces of the story that directly affect them. They don't see the effect of each piece on the organization as a whole – *they touch the elephant's leg and think they feel a tree trunk.* We need to equip our boards, management, and front-line staff with the tools they need to see the whole picture and tell the whole story within our organizations. When we do focus on the whole picture, we call it "systems thinking."

Smart executive directors take on the role of helping the whole system see the whole elephant. *They do not think they can see or hold the whole all by themselves.* They facilitate leadership in others and rely on the "whole system" to move the organization forward.

Successful organizations of the future will rely on executive directors, board members, and other leaders who:

- are highly self-aware;
- have strong communication skills;
- can coach others toward personal success;
- understand the leadership requirements of each life cycle of the organization;
- understand that different situations and phases of the life cycle will require different types of leadership;
- understand that if they have a predominant leadership style, the situation, times, or phase of their organization's life cycle may call for other types of leadership skills; and
- bring a full-systems approach to analyzing problems – reversing the culture of blame that prevails in many organizations (leaders too often blaming the staff, the board, or funders rather than looking at the whole system) and coaching the organization's partners toward a culture of shared accountability instead of individual finger-pointing.

Creating Boards of the Future

Selecting New Board Members for Partnership, not Power

Current thinking in nonprofit board development suggests selecting board members for their personal attributes, communication skills, and deep concern for the mission of the agency instead of for their connections, specific skills, or areas of expertise – resources that might be better found through consultants or other experts. Consider approaching former clients or users of the organization's programs, people with expertise in the organization's key programs, and people who represent the organization's key constituents to serve on your board.

As with executive directors, the leadership requirements at the governance level are not static. Different types of board members are required at different phases of the organization's life cycle. It is advisable to keep in mind where the organization is headed over the next three year cycle and to seek out leaders with skills that will match the organization's strategic priorities. There are some attributes, however, that are universally appealing in a board member, including:

- humility;
- a sense of humor;
- an ability to see the big picture;
- emotional maturity;
- a balanced approach;
- good communication skills; and
- the ability to think strategically.

Another trend in the board selection process is to turn nomination committees into board development committees. Instead of creating grids that list skills and attributes being sought, board development committees are charged with creating a balanced and diverse board, seeking people with the qualities listed above.

Board development committees are charged with taking stock of and understanding the phases of the organization's life cycle, noting whether it is new and entrepreneurial, in need of management and systems, in an expansion mode, or collaborating strategically with all its stakeholders and potential partners. Board development committees also need to assess the current strengths and weaknesses of the board, define gaps, and ensure succession on the board.

Characteristics to Be Considered by Board Development Committees

The following list includes characteristics that board development committees may wish to consider in building a committed and knowledge-able board and volunteer corps.

A. Understanding of the role of governance:

- has demonstrated an understanding of our mission;
- understands that he or she is working for the collective good;
- does not bring a personal agenda;
- is joining to further the mission, not the self;
- understands and is willing to sign a conflict of interest policy;
- understands the importance of respecting defined communication channels and will not undercut the authority of the executive director; and
- will work to create appropriate channels of communication and accountability feedback loops for staff, clients and the community.

B. Demographics:

- geographic; (Does the candidate represent areas we serve?)
- racial and/or ethnic diversity;
- gender;
- age; or
- other demographics that are important at this time in our organization's stage of development.

C. Skills and expertise:

- good listening skills;
- ability to facilitate dialogue and open discussion;
- good negotiating skills; (Works towards win/win situations versus "being right.")
- work or volunteer experience in "teams";
- real life experience with what our mission is about;
- fund development experience or willingness to participate;
- strategic or long-range planning experience;
- human resources management skills;
- nonprofit financial management ability;
- good people skills;
- board development experience; and/or
- organizational development experience.

Other categories to consider:

- prospective major donor;
- philanthropic reputation; and
- sense of humor.

Recruiting New Board Members

When recruiting new board members, the board development committee should strike a balance between begging for potential members and giving board candidates the third degree. In general, board development committees should do the following:

- Develop (and revisit annually) a policy statement for how the board will partner with the executive director, staff, and community. This statement should set the tone and parameters of the board's role and responsibilities. All new board members should understand the policy – which reflects the board's culture and style – to ensure that their personal values and styles are aligned with those of the organization.
- Develop a generic board member job description that allows prospective board members to clearly understand the expectations of the organization and what they can expect in return.
- Develop an overall profile of the current priorities and core work of the board over the next several years, including the types of people and attributes that will help the organization make progress on its priorities.

- Develop a matrix that will help the board identify candidates who reflect the organization's mission, vision, values, and current priorities.
- Develop a process – as formal or informal as needed to match the culture of the organization – for reviewing individual candidates and ensuring they are a good match for the organization.

Special Considerations when Recruiting Board Members

- Friends of the executive director or board members do not necessarily make good board members. Keep in mind that their presence can create subtle partnerships and boundary issues, as well as hamper the ability to confront openly and honestly.
- Stacking the board with relatives of board members can open the organization to accusations of nepotism and conflict of interest.
- While it can be great to have board members with professional skills (attorneys, accountants, etc.) who can help the organization, keep in mind that some may simply want to do board work to get away from their jobs. When board members do provide pro bono services to the organization, it should be clear that they are acting as any other volunteer; they do not speak or act for the board unless the full board expressly empowers them to do so.
- Tokenism is not real diversity. Avoid bringing on people simply because they fit a demographic profile; it is an insult to true diversity work. We do not mean that boards should remain homogeneous, but we believe it is better for boards to struggle through real discussions about who has power and control in their organizations and why, so that they can appreciate the fact that diversity enhances their organization. Board members need to outline how other important constituencies can gain access to and share power. Taking the time to design thoughtful, long-term strategies to recruit and orient new members is better than superficially changing the makeup of the board without addressing the underlying lack of understanding of true diversity.

Further Considerations for Effective Recruitment

- Create a board structure that asks potential board members to serve as committee members first. The benefits are twofold: you get to see prospects in action, and they get to see how the organization works before making a deeper commitment.
- Fully orient new board members into the culture of the organization, and explain the board's partnership with the executive director.
- Assign new board members a "buddy" from the existing board to help with orientation through the first few meetings.
- Have candidates come to the organization's office or workplace to meet the frontline staff. Keep in mind that if potential members do not have time to get to know the real work of the organization before committing to their governance role, they will not have time once they are board members.

Orienting New Board Members

New board members should visit the agency one more time for a full orientation to the board's bylaws and the organization's personnel policies, fundraising activities, fiscal procedures, and programs. A tour of the facilities and meeting with staff and constituents is most beneficial in helping new board members see the "whole elephant." The executive director should compile a board handbook that contains at least most of the following items:

- mission statement;
- conflict of interest policy (and any other policies to be signed by the board member);
- fact sheet (one to two pages – an overview of the agency);
- bylaws (a synopsis of key points is nice for new board members);
- list of dates and locations of board meetings;
- list of dates and locations of committee meetings;
- annual calendar or program schedule;
- board member responsibilities (job description);
- committee job descriptions;

- up-to-date board roster (name, address, telephone/fax, e-mail);
- certificate or review of board members liability insurance;
- copies of current policies, such as personnel policies, that the board approves;
- prospective board member referral form
- list of all major funding contracts (name of funder, amount, program funded);
- sample or draft of grant proposal;
- ample of solicitation letter with contribution response envelopes;
- section for board/committee meeting minutes;
- information packet (a separate packet that includes: brochure, annual report, contribution benefits brochure, press releases and articles, bumper stickers, business cards, etc.);
- communication guidelines (meeting guidelines and protocols for communication with the executive director, staff, press, public and board officers); and
- other appropriate materials.

The board president and the members of the board development committee should make an extra effort to ensure that a new board member feels very welcome at his or her first meeting. Make it clear that new members should feel comfortable asking for clarification of items they will likely not understand at first. Keep in mind that the "alphabet soup" that many nonprofits employ, common use of terms used in the field, budget definitions, voting procedures that may not be clear, and name-dropping by board members may make people feel excluded and out of their league when they first come on a board.

Board Orientation Checklist

The new board member has met with the development committee to go over:

- ☑ mission and values;
- ☑ how the mission is used as a screen for making decisions;
- ☑ future strategies;
- ☑ board development activities;
- ☑ expectations of board members;
- ☑ written board member job description;
- ☑ type of partnership expected of board members with other stakeholders, including executive director, staff, clients, and community;
- ☑ conflict of interest policy (including signature);
- ☑ fund development policies (expectation that all board members give within their means);
- ☑ any other board policies; and
- ☑ board decision-making policies.

The new board member has met with the executive director to:

- ☑ tour the facilities,
- ☑ meet the staff, and
- ☑ hear about day-to-day operations, including an overview of programs, finances, and fundraising, and for a brief overview of the personnel policies.

The New Work of the Board: Revisiting Board Meetings

One of the more important differences between the "old work" and the "new work" of the board is how board meetings themselves are conducted. In the old style, board meetings were process-driven, the agenda didn't vary much, committees routinely reported old business, and the emphasis was on information sharing.

Consider this: A board member who spends time going over changes in the minutes from the last meeting or asking for detail on a $1,000 line item within a million-dollar budget does not understand the true "oversight" nature of governance. Some people love to focus on detail, which can be a marvelous attribute in its proper place. But *attention to detail is not the job of a board member.* Meetings should be structured to allow board members to focus on what really matters, not on operational questions concerning facilities, people management, and budget minutiae. If you, as the executive director, are encouraging small-stakes "operational discussions," honestly assess whether you are doing it to encourage less involvement, less partnering, and less input on what really matters to your organization.

Teaching an Old Board New Work

Old Work	New Work
1 Management defines problems, assesses options, and proposes solutions. Board listens, learns, approves, and monitors.	1 Board and management discover issues that matter, mutually determine agenda, and solve problems together.
2 Board sets policy, which management implements. Respective territories are sharply defined; there is little or no border traffic. Domains are decided by organizational chart.	2 Board and management both set policy and implement it. Lines are blurred, borders are open. Domains are decided by nature of issue at hand.
3 Structure of standing committees parallels administrative functions. Premium is on permanent structure, established routines. Members occupy functional niches. Board maintains busy work.	3 Structure of board mirrors institution's strategic priorities. Premium is on flexibility, ad hoc arrangements. Members occupy functional intersections. Board creates centers of action.
4 Board meetings are process driven. Protocol doesn't vary. Function follows form. Emphasis is on transmission of information and reports.	4 Board meetings are goal driven. Protocol varies with circumstances. Form follows function. Emphasis is on participation and action.
5 Board is a collection of stars. It recruits people with an eye to expertise and status. The CEO cultivates individual relationships and exploits each trustee's talents.	5 Board is a constellation. It recruits team members with an eye to personality and overall chemistry. Board cultivates group norms and collective capabilities of trustees.

What *really matters in the board room* is using the volunteer time of the board member as if it were sacred. Use it to define and tackle strategic priorities, bringing to bear the collective wisdom of the board community to complement (and at times contradict) the staff's insider view.

Consider organizing board meetings so that substantive conversations and decisions can be made about finances, fundraising, governance, and the agency's strategic priorities. Consider setting up an annual calendar that enables the board to spend the majority of a meeting on one or two topics. Pro-forma reports from the executive director or the treasurer can be sent via e-mail or surface mail ahead of time, giving members an opportunity to ask questions if they have them without sitting through a verbal report.

For example, board meeting time spent considering fund development should focus strategically on relationship-building and the organization's viability, not on what the invitation to the next event should look like. Fundraising does not have to be revisited during every single board meeting if the board has had a substantive discussion of how it will meet its fiduciary responsibility in the current year and for the next few years. Ask a few board members (and development staff, where they exist) to bring an annual fund development plan to the board for discussion.

Guidelines for Nonprofit Boards

- *Create a code of ethics* for board members (see the Appendix for a sample) in order to address conflicts systematically and to serve as a strong reminder to people on the board that they are there to serve the mission of the organization. The existence of an ethics code sends a clear message to board and staff that they are accountable to high standards of conduct.

- *Focus on the mission.* Practice mission-focused management so that the mission permeates all of the major decisions and actions of the organization. A clear understanding of the organization's purpose will help create a team spirit and a common ground from which to build communication.

- *Talk!* Communicate openly about roles in the organization. Understand that roles change as the organization grows and as leaders transition out of the organization. Become aware of your own learning curve and how it affects your role. Make sure newer people are listening and learning and that experienced leaders are training new leaders. Lack of role definition between the board and the executive director is a chronic problem for many nonprofits; strike the right balance *for your organization* so that it can fulfill its mission and work efficiently toward its goals. Changes in key leadership should trigger a revisiting of roles – if a strong director departs, will the board step forward for awhile? Will it relax its oversight as the new director becomes acclimated?

- *Create sound policies that set parameters* for actions by each segment of the organization – the board, board committee, staff, executive director, volunteers, etc. A common weaknesses among boards is the creation of policies that are so tight, they result in micromanagement, or so loose, there isn't enough accountability. Policies should always be rooted in the mission and have a solid rationale. They should set *broad* parameters within which the director can manage and the staff can implement. Staff can be involved in setting policy through recommendations or by their presence on committees, but it is important for them to have the power to communicate with the board. Staff will more likely have more ownership over organizational policies if they have been involved in their development.

- *Handle leadership transitions carefully* by revisiting mission, values, and principal goals before proceeding with a major hiring or change in how the organization is structured. Keep in mind that when a founder or charismatic leader leaves the staff or board, *there will be a vacuum.* When a leader of any type leaves the organization, there is a period of transition. Good leaders plan for succession, but they cannot manage all the dynamics that change will bring. By reaffirming the mission and goals *and ensuring ongoing, clear communication,* a leader can lay a foundation that creates a clear set of expectations for the new director, staff, or board member.

- *Create an outcomes orientation.* The substantive work of the board is in working with staff, constituents, and the community to define real outcomes for the consumers of the organization's services, the community, and the field.

- *Create a future orientation.* The board should focus on larger trends in the environment, in the field, and in the community instead of concentrating on smaller day-to-day issues. The board should act as a window into the larger world for the staff and the organization, looking outward more and inward less.

- *Maintain absolute fidelity to constituents.* Some board members fail to see that governance is about others, not about themselves. Board members must act on behalf of those for whom the nonprofit is organized – the constituents – not the funders, not the staff, not the executive director, and not the board itself. Creating opportunities for dialogue with primary constituents is an important aspect of the board's responsibility.

- *Keep board members informed with relevant information* that reflects the context of the organization. Board members need information about the constituency, the field of endeavor, and the funding environment. Material and articles on relevant subjects should be circulated constantly. Consider establishing study groups and mini-seminars on matters of particular strategic relevance.

- *Reserve board meetings for work that has meaning.* Laundry lists of reports and information-sharing take valuable meeting time and energy away from board dialogue on core concerns and the board's own work plan.

- *Help the board find its own path of continuous improvement* to enhance its capacity for self-awareness, reflection, and honesty. Move away from a pure nominations committee toward a board development committee that doesn't exist simply to fill vacancies, but also sees to the health of the board and keeps it on track by evaluating, challenging, and developing long-range recruitment plans. Yes, board members should have connections and skills, but they should also be present on the board for the right reasons, including:
  - a personal mission that fits within and complements the mission of the organization;
  - the potential to be a good team member;
  - a willingness to engage in productive conversation;
  - a willingness to be accountable and see the whole system for what it is;
  - the ability to partner effectively with other stakeholders; and
  - a belief that the collective good is more important than personal power and control.
- *Create and adhere to fiscal procedures.* Recruit a strong treasurer who can fulfill the board's job description. Keep in mind that oversight does not mean micromanagement of the budget or its line items; rather, oversight means setting sensible policies within which the director and staff can act. Board liability is particularly high in this area because the public trusts board members to use tax dollars and donations wisely and for the purposes defined in an organization's documents. It is hard to recover the trust of the public if fiscal mismanagement is apparent.
- *Create a system for feedback* about programs from consumers, community, staff, and volunteers. This can be done through direct observation by board members, tracking program results by staff, and surveying consumers. Whatever the method, listening to feedback, especially from consumers and communities, gives yet another important perspective on your activities, lessens fear of "otherness," and makes the organization more "open" to the public.
- *Evaluate the executive director* and ensure that the director is evaluating staff and holding them accountable for their roles as stakeholders in meeting the mission. Evaluation is *the* accountability tool and the best way for you to know how accountable the director is to the mission and other stakeholders. Because performance evaluation can be difficult, it helps to have clear expectations and policies. Performance evaluation can be achieved by a small, representative group from the board, but it should occur regularly, not as a response to a crisis. Performance evaluations should be put in writing. Consider making your process for evaluating the executive director consistent with how other staff evaluations are handled in the organization. We encourage the development of a mutually respectful and systematic process for soliciting staff input as an important part of building communication skills and a culture of honest feedback.
- *Create a culture of openness to information, communication, and inclusiveness.* At the heart of many accountability problems – and many nonprofit problems in general – are poor communication skills or personal styles that run contrary to inclusiveness. Information should flow in all directions: up-down, down-up, and across. All stakeholders should be encouraged to address problems directly as they arise. Open communication will go a long way toward creating a functional and emotionally healthy organization.
- *Create a culture of diversity.* Organizations shortchange themselves when they neglect to recruit board members who are different from the majority. Diversity of background brings diversity of perspective. Diversity is another form of accountability. If you fear certain groups, such as constituents or wealthy people, examine your fears. Find out why you fear them, whether the

fear is real, and whether it is keeping the organization from knowing these people. Keep in mind that your organization will be richer, intellectually and spiritually, by casting a wider net.

- *Educate the board and staff to the key responsibility of holding the public trust.* While we may be dedicated to our mission, we often forget that by its tax-exempt nature the nonprofit board has stewardship over a particular public trust. Help staff and individual board members understand why the board exists.

- *Define ways in which the board, executive director, and staff formally communicate.* Consider such concerns as:

  - who informs when issues reach critical junctures;
  - who provides the board with timely information; and
  - how staff is involved in setting policy and making decisions.

Communication is a learned skill; organizations can encourage growth of this skill with systems that facilitate communication among their stakeholders.

- *Define who is accountable when communication breaks down.* Poor communication is a major reason for lack of organizational accountability; the board and staff must discuss how it will hold itself and others responsible for not adhering to the standards of communication, such as timely reports, attending meetings, providing supervision, etc.

- *Enhance opportunities for constituency feedback and empowerment.* Conduct needs assessments and encourage community people or consumers to join the board. Staying in touch with the people and the community served helps create a culture of openness and a focus on the mission and goals for the broader community.

- *Provide accessibility to the organization, to the media, government, and donors.* Organizational transparency and a culture of openness demonstrate to the public that you are accountable and have nothing to hide.

FUND DEVELOPMENT

CHAPTER 7

We owe a debt of gratitude to Kim Klein. Her teachings inform our fund development practice to such an extent that our writings echo much of what we have learned from her.

– Third Sector New England

What does the executive director need to know about fund development? Just about everything! Fund development is one of the most critical of an executive director's functions; without funding, nothing else in the organization can move forward.

This chapter focuses on an overview of the fund development basics – particularly for executive directors who double as development staff in smaller nonprofits. We'll explore:

- how to set up a development plan;
- how to manage the transition to more complex fundraising efforts; and
- the role of the executive director and the board of directors.

The Good Practice Basics

Raising resources for nonprofits is about discipline, planning, passion for the mission, and knowing how to connect people to that mission. Good practice basics in fund development can be summed up as an upward spiral of communication, planning, doing, and asking.

To maintain this upward spiral, the executive director must:

- maintain or build a healthy organization with a relevant mission;
- develop a case for support based on organizational relevance;
- identify others who have an interest in the work of the organization;
- plan how to contact current and potential donors;
- position volunteers and staff to "ask" for support;
- carry out the plan;
- evaluate the fundraising efforts; and
- build a better fund development program based on the information collected.

Fundraising is the act of asking for money, whether through face-to-face meetings, direct mail, special events, proposals to foundations, or responding to requests for proposals from government sources. The act of asking for money is only one component of fund development.

Fund development is the ongoing strategic positioning of an organization to sustain and grow its resources by building multiple relationships with those who understand and care about the organization's relevance to the community. Building these relationships requires creating a shared vision, clear articulation of mission, creative strategies, and a solid communication plan. (See chapter 8, **Public Relations.**)

The first steps in fund development – for all organizations, no matter what size – are:

- making the case for support, and
- finding the resources.

Making the Case for Support

1. Describe your organization's relevance to its community in terms of mission, purpose, vision, and need.
2. Align the organization's inner circle – the staff, board, and volunteers – around the mission and vision of the organization.[1]
3. Define the key strategies, programs, and activities for fulfilling your mission.
4. Make clear the connection between the organization's core cause and relevance to the community and the interests of your current and potential donors, as well as the interests of other community stakeholders.
5. List all the resources that will be required to implement strategies, programs, and activities; include in this list the people (paid staff and volunteers) that are needed, the time they will spend, the equipment and facilities they will need, and the administrative overhead that will be attributed to running the project.

[1] See Chapter 2, **Mission, Vision, and Values,** and Chapter 13, **Managing Change,** for tips on how to align key stakeholders with a shared understanding of the organization's relevance and meaning to the community it serves.

6 Assign a cost to all of the resources. (This is your budget.)

7 Determine (internally and informally) how you will know and be able to show that you have accomplished what you set out to do. This begins the evaluation process – a key component of overall organizational and fund development since it confirms why the agency is relevant to the public it is intended to serve.

One of the most important roles of the executive director in fund development is defining the organization's relevance to the community. The executive director must be skilled at communicating this relevance with integrity, credibility, and passion in order to build genuine relationships with those who will care and contribute.

Finding the Resources

Fundraising is like an iceberg. Most of our attention goes to the tip – asking for money – instead of to the mammoth structure lurking below the surface. Sound fund development plans are built on top of two main factors: relationships that continuously strengthen connections between people and the mission of the organization and solid organizational structures and practices that enable the organization to carry out its mission effectively. Both take considerable time and effort, but since they are the foundation of the fundraising effort, adequate attention must be paid to them.

The executive director's role changes with the size of the organization. In organizations that are large enough to employ development staff, the executive director will be most responsible for "making the case" in partnership with the board and staff and for overseeing the work of the development staff in developing the fund development plan. In smaller organizations, the executive director will do it all, with the support and participation of the board.

A fund development plan should define, in detail, how the organization will identify potential sources of funding and donors, what communication methods and tools will be used, which activities need to be implemented, when it will all take place, and how much it will cost.

The basic steps for creating a fund development plan include the following:

1 Make time to plan.

The first step is to set aside time to plan and then plan some more. Do not be afraid to spend quality time on planning. Remember that the act of asking donors for money is just the tip of the iceberg. Every event the organization hosts, every proposal sent to foundations, and every ad book produced should be part of an overall strategic effort that the organization has thought out in advance.

2 Start with a budget.

Once a case has been made, it is time to create a budget that shows the cost of doing business for a particular program or for the entire organization. This budget is different from the organization's operating budget. It should be future-oriented and should describe the full funding needs of the programs. Keep in mind that since programs are not always fully funded, the actual budget may differ from the fundraising budget. The fundraising budget should show all the costs that would be incurred realistically if the program were fully funded. This is how you know how much money you want to raise.

3 Survey the funding field.

Define all the different ways in which the agency can raise funds: foundations, corporations, government contracts, individuals (reached through face-to-face meetings, direct mail, events, telephone, the Internet, and door-to-door canvassing).

4 Examine your capacity.

Base current plans on an honest evaluation of the previous fundraising effort. It is important to be absolutely realistic, maybe even conservative, about the agency's capacity to implement each aspect of the plan. Note whether there have been changes in the staff, board leadership, or funding environment (changes in the economy, competing campaigns, shifts in foundation priorities, etc.) that will affect your effort. Determine how involved the board will be in implementing the plan. Take the time to research and test assumptions for new techniques that have not been tried by the organization.

5 Narrow the list.

After researching assumptions, critiquing previous performance, and scanning the internal and external environment, narrow the list of fundraising methods to a realistic few. Choose those that will bring in the most funding for the least effort, while simultaneously building a broader and deeper funding base.

Continuously work to diversify funding sources and to deepen current donor interest in the cause. Fundraising efforts (especially time-consuming or low-yield events) that do not broaden or deepen the donor base should be discarded.

6 Create a calendar.

Fit each fundraising method and event into a calendar that shows when each one will take place. Backing up from the day(s) of the event, fill in the timeline for implementation. Be sure to include time for planning and for developing related materials such as invitations or media packets, as well as the actual ask and the necessary follow-up.

7 Evaluate each step.

Evaluate each technique and measure it against goals to determine (at a minimum) whether:

- the technique reflects the organization's mission and values;
- the net gain was worth the effort put in;
- the funding base was broadened; and
- the funding base was deepened.

Who Gives, Anyway? And Why?

While the government gives the greatest share of the dollars going for social services, arts, housing, and health, *individuals give 85 percent* of the nongovernmental charitable contributions in the United States. Individuals give *directly* to causes that matter to them by writing a check, establishing a trust, creating a private foundation, participating in fundraising events, or creating estate gifts in their wills, and *indirectly* through their share of the tax dollars that fund government contracts or by contributing to community foundations and pooled giving programs.

Surprisingly, *foundations and corporations account for only 15 percent* of the nongovernmental charitable giving in the United States. Executive directors and fund development staff, however, often labor under the illusion that most of the money available for charitable purposes will come from foundations and corporations. As a result, they spend a disproportionate amount of time and effort trying to generate funds from foundations and corporations that typically focus on special projects, have a myriad of strings attached, and generally serve as short-term sources of funding.

Most executive directors and fund development staff would be better off spending more of their time cultivating gifts from individuals, who tend to attach fewer strings to their gifts and to be involved over a longer term, giving nonprofit organizations more autonomy and stability in providing programs that are client- and community-driven. Not that it is easy to develop an individual giving program, but those who put time and effort into creating one are usually pleased with the flexibility it gives them in the long run.

Typically, individuals tend to give 45 percent of their contributions to religious institutions[2] and distribute the remaining 55 percent to other nonprofit organizations, according to the following breakdown:

- educational (11%)
- undesignated (10%)
- human services (9%)
- health (8%)
- arts and humanities (7%)
- public/society benefit (4%)
- environmental (2%)
- international (1%)
- other (3%)

Looking at the list, it is clear that religious organizations are by far the most successful at raising funds from individuals. Among human service agencies, the Salvation Army is usually among the best. If we think about what the two groups have in common, there are several lessons we can draw:

[2] Figures are taken from Fundraising for Social Change by Kim Klein (Inverness: Chardon Press, 1994) – the most important book on fundraising that every small and mid-sized community-based nonprofit should own.

- *Ask frequently.* If you don't ask, you won't receive. Religious organizations tend to ask for donations on a weekly basis, with periodic requests for special collections. During the winter holidays, Salvation Army bell-ringers are often asking at every street corner.
- *Ask in person.* People tend to respond at higher rates when they are asked in person, even by a stranger. Americans, especially, find it hard to say no to a request made in person. Statistics show that fewer than 1 percent respond to a first-time direct mail appeal whereas requests made in person yield a 50 percent return.
- *Build relationships, trust, and visibility.* Churches constantly work at building relationships with their constituents, imparting their message, and creating a vision and feeling of community. The Salvation Army's holiday appeal creates visibility, name recognition, and a sense of fellowship. Visibility backed up by trustworthy practices and sound programs is crucial to fundraising success.
- *Build relevance to donors.* For centuries, religious institutions have used the concept of "exchange" to present the value of their service to the people who can support it. They have done so without shame because they believe fervently in the value of their service to humankind. Their constituents, for the most part, value this exchange and give generously.
- *Produce value.* All viable, credible nonprofits produce value – or a product. The product may be improved education, safer neighborhoods, less cruelty to animals, better access to health, more performing arts, or a cleaner environment. Because these products add value, people can be found who care about them and are willing to make an exchange for them. That exchange may be in the form of time (volunteerism), goods and services (in-kind gifts), and/or money (every week for some churches).

People give out of self-interest, however broadly defined. They exchange their contributions and donations for the value produced for the common good by the nonprofit organization.

Successful fundraisers understand the principle of the "exchange" and never underestimate the value the donor receives in exchange for their gift.

The Importance of Building Relationships

The executive director's most essential role is to provide leadership in fund development:

- *Define the organization's relevance to the community. Spread* the message through written materials, such as direct mail letters, newsletters, major gift or special campaign packages, fact sheets that address "frequently asked questions," and acknowledgment programs.
- *Build relationships with the staff, board, volunteers, donors, clients, and community. Work* to ensure that everyone associated with the organization understands its relevance and value to the community. *Create* organizational transparency so that everyone can see and understand how the organization functions. *Network* with peers in the field, other nonprofit leaders, public policy makers, civic leaders, business leaders, philanthropists, people who work for philanthropists, investment advisors, and trust attorneys. *Develop* contacts that provide feedback on ideas, offer collaboration, open doors, and generate interest in your programs in the right places and with the right people.
- *Communicate the value the nonprofit adds to society. Promote* the value the organization adds to society. *Foster* understanding of the exchange or value – albeit not always tangible – that people get from their donation to the nonprofit. *Create* opportunities for getting the message out through special events that raise public awareness and create name recognition; press conferences that address new issues, facts, or services; hosting important meetings; or special training that you provide.
- *Create additional opportunities to promote and request. Explain* the value of the organization and *ask* for support through special year-end promotions for tax benefits, donor cards that provide opportunities to make multiyear pledges, and gifts in memory of, or gifts in honor of, friends or relatives.

Keep in mind that relationship-building, networking, and communicating are all forms of donor research. Asking peers and board members is the quickest way to identify and build a profile of potential donors in the business, foundation, investment, and government funding worlds.

Identifying Individual and Institutional Donors

Successful fundraising depends on disciplined, hard work and adherence to some proven principles of fund development. It boils down to researching and list-building.

Research

Fundraising research can seem endless – government funding must be unearthed; corporate and foundation giving programs must be found and reviewed; and lists of individual donor prospects must be developed. If the organization has development staff, research is their job, and the executive director should review their results on a regular basis. If the executive director carries the fundraising function, keep in mind that research is an essential aspect of planning.

Research begins with a review of current donors. To get a good sense of the current situation, ask the following questions:

- Who gives to the organization and why?
- What percentage of donors are active?
- What percentage of donors have lapsed?
- Where do the donors live?
- Why do the donors care about the organization?
- Which methods of fundraising have been most successful at reaching these donors?
- How can others who match the current donor profile be reached?

Researching the funding priorities of foundations and corporations will help the executive director or fund development staff avoid wasting time chasing funding sources that are unlikely to be fruitful. For foundations and larger corporations with giving programs:

- Call and get their guidelines and annual report.
- Review the guidelines and annual report carefully to find out the mission of the organization, the type of groups it supports, the number and size of the grants, and the overall giving budget.
- Record the deadline and application procedures.

List-Building

Even the smallest, most grassroots organization can find new people to add to its prospective donor list. Think about every contact that you make in the course of the day, week, month, and year, and you will begin to see that you come in contact with potential donors virtually every single day. As you build your list, have it reviewed by people who may know more about the individuals on it and can give you advice on how to approach them to begin or increase their giving. To start or add to your list:

- Include all current donors. Often, current donors would be willing to increase their gift, if only they were asked.
- Reach out to vendors, friends, neighbors, and constituents for support and for the names of others who should be asked.
- Ask current donors who are particularly close to the agency, as well as board members and other executive directors to suggest people who should be included.
- Call, get on the mailing lists of, and check the websites of key foundations, corporations, and government agencies that could become funders.
- Ensure that the agency is represented at meetings where funding information is exchanged; join organizations to meet potential sponsors and funders.
- Create donor network trees (or ask development staff to do so) that connect the dots among the people who know each other, socialize, worship, or work together. Identifying the connections between potential donors and current friends of an organization is important for laying the groundwork for major gift or capital campaigns.

Places to Find Information

Associated GrantMakers of Massachusetts (AGM), located at 55 Court Street in Boston *(www.agmconnect.org)* is an invaluable place for novice and expert fundraisers to research information. AGM maintains a library of development periodicals and publishes the *Massachusetts Grantmakers Guide,* which includes information on over 300 foundation, family, and corporate trusts in Massachusetts.

The Division of Public Charities at the Massachusetts Office of the Attorney General maintains current financial and background information on all charitable organizations, including trusts, foundations, and other nonprofits operating in the Commonwealth.

The Catalog of Federal Domestic Assistance contains hundreds of assistance programs administered by federal agencies. It is available on line at: http://www.cfda.gov or by mail from: Superintendent of Documents, PO Box 371954, Pittsburgh, PA 15250-7954. Call 202-708-5126 for more information.

The Federal Register contains requests for proposals for proposed and approved rules and regulations for federal domestic assistance programs. It is online at: http://www.access.gpo.gov/su_docs/aces/aces140.html. Call: (888) 293-6498 or fax: (202) 512-1262 for more information.

Public libraries are another great source of information on potential funders.

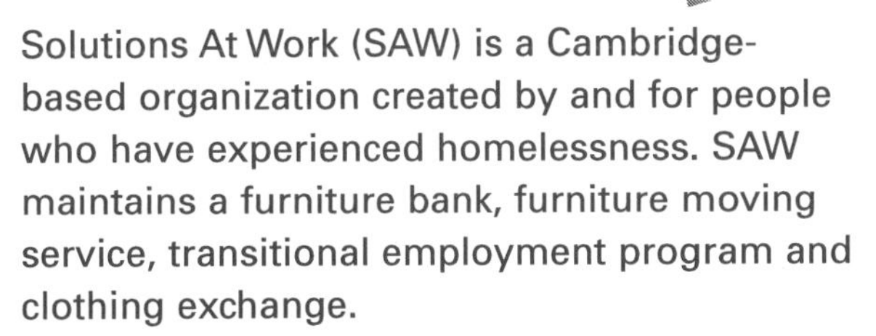

Case Study: Solutions At Work

Solutions At Work (SAW) is a Cambridge-based organization created by and for people who have experienced homelessness. SAW maintains a furniture bank, furniture moving service, transitional employment program and clothing exchange.

In the mid-1990s, SAW received a technical assistance grant to hire a consultant to work with members to create their first fund development plan. Their aim was to create a plan that would allow them to cultivate a diversified fundraising base. At that time, they were operating with a budget of less than $50,000. Five years later, the budget has grown to almost $300,000 and strategies have been put in place for it to increase to half a million dollars over the next two years.

The executive director recognizes the importance of relationship-building and has worked collaboratively with other homeless-led organizations (including doing joint fundraisers), with community religious groups, with local community foundations in Cambridge and Boston, and with the business sector.

Prior to the technical planning that allowed SAW to revamp fund development efforts, funding came mostly from foundations. As part of the planning effort, SAW developed a stronger board of directors and created a plan that would draw upon local individual support, major donors, and foundation, corporate, religious and government funding. Recognizing the need to stabilize the funding base before the organization could go forward, SAW made a strong (and successful) pitch for more foundation support, which allowed time to develop other strategies. At the same time, SAW strengthened public relations efforts and was fortunate enough to be highlighted on the "Today" show on Thanksgiving Day in 1996 – an opportunity which brought in new individual donations.

At that time, SAW also began sending out mailings. The first list was made up of people and organizations that had previously donated furniture to the furniture bank. The mailings were done by hand, and donors were thanked with lovely, heartfelt letters from formerly homeless leaders within the organization. Board members were asked to mail to their friends.

This modest effort was the beginning of a successful fundraising strategy. Currently, SAW adds names to its mailing list by keeping track of furniture bank donors, and event participants, and by gathering names at various community affairs. SAW's funding base now includes individual donors, local and federal government funding, corporations, religious organizations, private foundations, small events and earned income from the furniture bank and transitional employment. Recently, fundraising letters were sent to college classmates of the executive director, garnering a large gift from the family foundation of one classmate – hence proving the potential link between direct mail and major gifts. SAW now receives $45,000 annually from individual donors – almost the total budget of five years ago.

Sources of funding for SAW

	1999	1998	1997
Corporate	$ 5,369	$ 7,900	$21,000*
Foundation	134,000	129,000	102,000
Individual	47,000	40,477	40,000
Faith-based	11,500	9,873	20,000*
Fees/moving	22,000	25,000	19,000
Govt. contract	30,000	30,000	3,700
Special event	5,000	18,000	5,000

*In 1997, corporate and faith-based gifts were particularly high because a special campaign to buy a truck for the furniture bank.

SAW's goal was to build on the relationships made during the campaign and steadily increase donations in each area. In 2000, the organization focused on corporate donations, and raised more in the first six months than they had all year in 1999.

SAW has also gained greater support from family foundations. They did this by working closely with the Cambridge Community Foundation and by ensuring they were listed at the Boston Foundation so that the organization and its mission and programs can be reviewed by donors who make designated grants. Currently, they are researching other family foundations in an effort to expand this source.

By making sure that their income sources are mixed, SAW keeps from becoming too dependent on any one source. In addition, this diversity has helped the organization gain skills in a variety of fundraising techniques. Developing a solid plan implemented with consistent follow-through has been the key to their incremental, but successful, growth in resources.

SAW also credits increased attention to public relations. They have received good media coverage – in local papers, on the Today Show and with a recent story on CNN. SAW makes their uniqueness work to their advantage in public relations and in crafting their message to donors. Staff and board do, however, see a need for creating a stronger, more consistent public relations plan as part of the organization's development plan.

Another area that they find needs constant attention is developing adequate people power. In their small organization, the burden for fundraising and public relations has tended to fall on the executive director and other staff, with some board support. They now have a fundraising chair on the board and recognize that they need to hire a staff person dedicated to fundraising. While they used to leave it to luck, SAW now consciously designs mechanisms for bringing in fundraising volunteers and working with them.

They advise other small nonprofits to take advantage of free courses on fundraising, volunteer coordination and board development, as well as *to speak with others who have developed good approaches and systems.* They received free help in developing a marketing plan from the Community Consulting Team, which brings together graduates of business schools and selects six to ten nonprofits to work with each year.

Finally, SAW staff believe that, no matter how small the organization, a *website* is absolutely necessary for visibility. They believe that the Internet has become the way to access information and make connections. Their web address is: *(www.SAWork.org.)*

SAW summarizes the lessons they have learned as follows:

- Bring on volunteers who understand financial responsibility;
- Access all the free help and information you can from: area universities (they used Harvard Business School volunteer

programs extensively); community foundations; other nonprofits; the business community; and the faith community. Develop your list of questions and do not be afraid to go out and ask for help;

- Create a diversified fund development plan. Start with what you have (names of friends of board members may make up your initial direct mail list), follow your plan and build on each success;
- Thank donors;
- Communicate with donors about your programs and their relevance. SAW produces an informative, though brief, newsletter. They also send copies of important newspaper coverage to their donors; and
- Get a website and stay up-to-date with technology.

Basic Fundraising Techniques

Research and list-making are ongoing activities that must eventually be incorporated into *planning activities* that will eventually become *program activities* that will eventually lead to the actual *request for funding.* Fundraising techniques help prepare the agency to "ask" for money. A good fund development plan includes methods to reach a variety of targets; those targets may include *individuals, government sources, foundations, and corporations.*

Individual Donors

Individual donors provide the most money with the fewest strings attached. A future-oriented executive director will help lead the organization toward building a solid individual donor program. It may start small, but if the effort is continued and maintained, it can pay off handsomely down the road. Individual donors are generally reached through:

- face-to-face meetings during annual appeals and major gift programs;
- direct mail appeals;
- telemarketing, telethons, radio appeals;
- door-to-door canvassing;
- house parties or other smaller gatherings; and
- large-scale events.

The goal of all individual gifts programs is three-pronged: (1) to acquire new donors, (2) to retain these donors, and (3) to get these donors to give more over time.

There are several tried-and-true methods for acquiring new donors. Every nonprofit should build into its plan at least *one* of the following strategies:

- direct mail appeal targeted to a list of friends that was generated by board, staff, and others, followed by a telephone call or face-to-face meeting;
- direct mass mail appeal to lists of people who have contributed to similar causes;
- face-to-face meetings with potential donors;
- house parties; and
- telephone, e-mail, and other Internet-based appeals.

Direct Mail

Direct mail is one way to begin to build an individual giving program. Even though the increasing costs of printing, postage, and purchasing lists – coupled with a standard return rate of less than 1 percent on initial mailings – have somewhat diminished the attractiveness of the direct mail technique, it is still a viable method, particularly for organizations that lack a current donor base. The real appeal of direct mail comes with the knowledge that, of the donors who respond to the first mailing, two-thirds will give again. The cost of the first mailing should be viewed as the cost of acquiring a new donor; the actually funding comes in the second and subsequent mailings.

Nonprofits looking to cut the costs of using direct mail should consider trading lists with other agencies and developing internal lists made up of names given by board members, staff, and others. It is a slower method, but the names will tend to be "hotter." If the board member (or other source of names) signs the request letter, the yield may be even higher than the 1 percent return that is considered standard for a "warm" list – one that is sent to people who have already given to a cause similar to yours.

It is important to do your homework before venturing into the world of direct mail. Learn about direct mail at seminars or through fundraising "how to" books. Collect direct mail samples from other nonprofits. Create a cost-benefit analysis (budget) of the cost of acquiring a new donor. Done right, direct mail will slowly, but surely, build a base of donors for your organization.

Personal Solicitation

Personal solicitation is a good method for raising gifts of $100 or more. It not only serves to help board members and other volunteers practice (and overcome their fear of) asking for money, it prepares them for asking for major gifts. The steps involved in personal solicitation include:

1. *Identifying prospects.* Create a list of people from your direct mail effort or from names suggested by board members and others. Review the list (with a small group of knowledgeable supporters) to make sure that each person meets the following qualifications:
   - they have the financial ability to make a gift within the range you have set;
   - you have evidence that they care about your cause; and
   - someone within your organizational family knows them well enough to approach them in person or sign a letter to them.
2. *Training volunteers to approach the prospects.* Volunteers should be trained on how to handle the telephone conversation and any face-to-face meetings. It is important for each volunteer to be comfortable discussing the organization and to be able to respond to questions about the organization; fact sheets are helpful. It is also important that each volunteer be comfortable responding to the various typical responses that prospective donors will make – from an outright "no" to "I need to check with my partner."
3. *Approaching prospects.* The standard approach is to send a letter signed by the volunteer to the prospective donor. The volunteer then calls the prospective donor and either asks for the gift over the telephone or asks for a meeting and solicits a gift at that time. At the time of the call or visit, the volunteer should be equipped with basic materials about the organization as well as a pledge card that allows a variety of donor options, such as paying by check or credit card, pledging over time, or making a gift in honor or memory of someone important to them.
4. *Following up with donors.* Obviously, as with all fundraising, donors should be thanked for their contribution. It is a good idea to thank those who said no to this request, but took the time to meet with a volunteer, for their time and interest; you never know what the future holds. It is also a good idea to thank your volunteers for helping out with the effort.

Government Sources

The size and availability of government grants and contracts can vary greatly depending on who controls the political agenda. During the 1980s, social service agencies in Massachusetts learned that lesson the hard way when their funds were cut across the board by 16 percent or more. Agencies that relied less on government resources – and had more experience finding other sources of funding – fared far better during that difficult time. While government funding may seem stable over a five-year period, it will not remain stable over the life of a nonprofit. Federal grants for nonprofits have been cut dramatically during the last two decades of the twentieth century.

Find out about the availability of government funding by getting on mailing lists, researching over the Internet, reading state and federal registers (also often available over the Internet), and talking with colleagues in your field. Joining statewide or national associations or coalitions is another good way of finding out about government resources that provide funding for your cause.

Foundations

Private, family, and community (local and national) foundations account for only 7 percent of all charitable giving. Foundations are generally good sources of support for new initiatives, and they often are willing to provide several years of funding to get the initiative off the ground. A few foundations are known for funding ongoing operations in particular fields, such as the arts, higher education, or social services, but these are rare and typically will not provide 100 percent of the operating costs of a single agency.

Foundation guidelines and giving limitations can be researched easily, using the Internet or regional associations of grant makers, or by calling for general information. Larger foundations have program staff that review proposals, make site visits, and write recommendations (usually in the form of a one page synopsis) to the foundation's trustees. In the largest foundations, program officers have areas of specialty, such as housing, economic development, education, international affairs, health, or the arts. In some foundations, the program officers do all the legwork, and the trustees make the final decision, while in others, the trustees merely rubber stamp staff recommendations. Either way, it is important to make the program officer's job as easy as possible. To do so:

- *Read* the guidelines of the foundation carefully; if the mission of your organization does not match the philanthropic mission of the foundation, don't waste their time or yours. Program officers at the biggest foundations often have several hundred proposals to review for each grant-making cycle.
- *Call* the foundation and try to speak directly to a program officer to introduce your proposal or to find out if your program matches their mission. Keep in mind that the staff is trained to be discouraging since often as few as 10 percent of submitted proposals are funded; so do not be disheartened. If the person you speak with, however, says that the program you have described is absolutely not a match, do not try to wedge a square peg into a round hole – you will only look desperate.
- *Learn* how to write a concise, easy-to-read proposal that is no longer than five to ten pages. Check with your regional nonprofit association for available training or refer to the sources listed in the bibliography. Ask an experienced grantwriter to review your proposal, then incorporate feedback in your proposal. Ask foundation staff for feedback on what was good or bad about the proposal you submitted to them.
- *Write* an executive summary, making it easier for the program officer to present your proposal for internal review.
- *Develop* realistic budgets. Keep in mind that program officers review proposals from all across the nonprofit sector and are familiar with reasonable salary ranges and the general costs of doing business. Do not inflate budgets.

Corporations

Although the trend is changing, only a small percentage of corporations have formal giving programs. While the concepts of cause-related marketing and promotion of social investment are growing, corporations are in business to make money, not give it away. Even the most socially conscious corporation is likely to give away no more than five percent of pre-tax profits; more typically, the amount is 2 percent of pre-tax profits. Larger corporations with community relations departments tend to make donations in ways similar to foundations – they usually request written proposals and have staff review them, make site visits, and make recommendations to the decision makers within the company.

Local businesses can be invaluable partners for nonprofit organizations by providing funds, lending meeting space, giving material goods, or providing volunteers. Local businesses are more likely to see the benefit of investing in their home community and can be approached through direct mail, telephone calls, door-to-door solicitations, or face-to-face appointments. Consider asking for larger donations to sponsor events or smaller contributions to advertise in event programs or ad booklets. Local businesses often will donate items for raffles and auctions, or provide printing services or food and supplies in exchange for publicity in some form, such as inclusion of the company name on banners, T-shirts, program books, annual reports, or agency newsletters.

Research local businesses and corporations through trade associations, the Chamber of Commerce, and by asking board members and others whom they know.

Major Gifts and Capital Campaigns

Major gifts programs are designed as part of an annual fundraising plan or as a special event. Capital campaigns are special one-time campaigns for raising funds to purchase a building, make capital improvements, or create an endowment. Major gifts and capital campaigns operate under the same basic principles outlined above for individual donors although the financial goal of the campaign will determine the levels of request that will be made. Individual donors will be asked to contribute at varying levels, according to their means.

The goal for a major gifts or capital campaign should not be simply picked out of the air or determined solely by what it would be nice to raise. The goal should be established by thoroughly researching the capacity of the identified prospects. Consider investing time and resources to conduct a feasibility study – either performed in-house or led by a consultant – for capital campaigns that have a goal of $1 million or more.

Several basic rules of fundraising have been established and confirmed as reasonable practice throughout the years, including:

- The 80/20 rule, which holds that 80 percent of the funds raised by individuals will come from 20 percent of the donors.
- The rule that you need three prospects for every gift – meaning three prospects who have the means to give at the level required, and that roughly one out of every three people asked will give. Ideally, try to have four prospects for every gift sought. For example, to obtain three gifts of $5,000, identify 9 to 12 people who have the means to give at that level and an interest in your organization or mission. Ask them in person.
- The rule that the largest single gift should equal 10 percent of the campaign goal.

Be sure to include your volunteers on your prospect list. One of the most frequent questions volunteers get asked is "How much did you give?" That's why all volunteers should be strongly encouraged to give a gift – preferably at the level at which they will be soliciting.

A gift range chart for a major gifts campaign to raise $50,000 might look like this:

Gift Range Chart

# of Gifts	Size of Gifts	Total	# of Prospects
1	$5,000	$ 5,000	3 - 4
2	$2,500	$ 5,000	6 - 8
5	$1,500	$ 7,500	15 - 20
10	$1,000	$10,000	30 - 40
15	$ 500	$ 7,500	45 - 60
20	$ 250	$ 5,000	60 - 80
100	$ 100	$10,000	300 - 400

In this sample campaign, approximately 30 to 40 volunteers should be recruited to ask the prospects in the $250 to $2,500 ranges for face-to-face meetings, which would require each volunteer to meet with about five prospects. The 300 prospects at the $100 level could be approached by letter, initially, and followed up with a telephone call.

Keep in mind that major gifts and capital campaigns should be *volunteer-driven.* The executive director and development staff can provide backup to the volunteers or may choose to participate in meetings where higher levels of gifts are being solicited, but cannot possibly be expected to meet with the number of people that must be approached over the course of a 10- to 12-week major donor drive. More importantly, peers give to peers – which is why your volunteer base should reflect your donor pool of prospects.

Remember, the work of the executive director is to *build the relationships* that encourage people to care enough about the organization and its mission to be willing to volunteer as fundraisers.

Fundraising Roles and Responsibilities

The Executive Director

Fund development is a crucial responsibility of the executive director. Although a deep understanding of the organization's field is essential, fund development, along with administration, financial oversight, and people management, comes with the territory.

An executive director in an organization *with* development staff should be spending at least 20 percent of the work week (one day) on fund development. In organizations where the executive director *doubles* as development staff, as much as 80 percent of the work week may be spent on development tasks.

In "small shop" organizations where a single development person carries multiple responsibilities, the executive director should be spending two to three days a week on development related activities. In larger organizations, where multiple development staff are responsible for writing proposals, running events, managing databases, and creating individual appeals, 20 percent of the executive director's time should be spent on meetings with donors, policy-makers, and foundation program staff. In these larger organizations, a key role of the development staff should be enabling the executive director to deliver the agency's core message in as many venues as possible.

The role of the executive director in fund development will change with the size and complexity of the organization. Nonetheless, as the executive director moves from being the "doer" of tasks to becoming the "facilitator" of staff and key volunteers, the ability to manage his or her time in order to spend enough time on fund development remains a key responsibility. Keep in mind that not allocating enough time for planning and attention to the tasks associated with fund development is *the major reason* that most organizations fail to meet fundraising goals.

Development Staff

Integrate development staff into the life of the agency – whether there is one part-time or five full-time staffers. Include them in strategic planning discussions and give them access to the board and other fundraising volunteers.

Orient development staff to all of the organization's programs. It is a good practice to have development staff actually engage in the core work of the agency – serving in the soup kitchen, staffing the opening of the art show, and answering the hotline – from time to time. This provides first-hand knowledge that allows staff to better communicate what the agency's programs really do and what is needed to get the job done. In addition, doing so allows front-line staff to see development staff as real people, not just as those who get their own office and the best computers – thus making them more open to helping the development staff when program statistics or extra volunteers are needed.

Development staff should have a commitment to the mission of the organization. They should be donors, within their means. They should understand the difference between fund development and fundraising. And they should be skilled at both.

Development staff should understand how to build organizational capacity by laying out realistic, achievable plans and facilitating implementation of the tasks within the plans in a timely fashion, drawing on the strengths of the executive director, board members, and other fundraising volunteers. In fact, their skill and experience in building this capacity should dictate their salary level.

All development people need strong communication skills that enable them to connect donors and prospects to the mission of the organization. They must also be forward-thinking, goal-oriented, and disciplined. Fundraising is hard work and is sometimes disappointing; high self-esteem, optimism, and perseverance are important attributes of a successful development staff.

An executive director who does not understand the complexity of developing a sustainable fund development program will inevitably make unreasonable demands on development staff. Development staffers are not money machines. They cannot be dictated a dollar amount to be raised without being provided the necessary support and direction for building the organizational capacity to reach goals.

Executive directors and boards need to view development staff as the people who help build the organization's capacity to attract and maintain donors and who enable them and their volunteers to "ask" on behalf of the organization.

Boards and executive directors should beware of development staff or consultants who market pure technique over long-term development practices, particularly when considering telemarketing – a field rife with unscrupulous operators. Avoid development people who start with blanket statements about how much money they can raise instead of talking about how they can help build the organization's capacity to raise funds in a variety of ways.

Development staff, executive directors, and board members should concentrate on developing plans that build on the organization's current donor base and successful fundraising techniques. Avoid development people or consultants who suggest plans or techniques that do not incorporate and build upon existing donors and strategies. The executive director must ensure that development staff walk their talk and aren't simply style over substance. Building organizational capacity and solid relationships takes hard, sustained work.

The Board of Directors

The buck stops with the board of directors. Board members, ultimately, have responsibility for the organization. They set the parameters that ensure the organization solicits funds honestly and responsibly, and they provide the oversight that ensures funds are raised at a level that will support operations and are spent responsibly.

Every nonprofit organization should have an expectation that each board member will contribute to its future viability in some way. Board members should donate both time and money (within their means). They should also work at building the relationships that will sustain the organization over time. Board members must take a leadership role in fund development because they are legally responsible for the organization's health and well-being.

Some nonprofits employ a "give, get, or get off the board" attitude with board members. But fund development and board development are never so starkly black and white. Many nonprofits can benefit greatly from board members who are unable to contribute financially. Both fund development and board development are processes in motion that require flexibility and growth. The bottom line still remains, however, that if a board member – who is legally and morally responsible for the nonprofit organization – will not contribute to and participate in the planning for the organization's future, then why should anyone else?

A good fund development plan – even for a very small nonprofit, needs many people to succeed. The executive director and board must act as partners in growing their organization's fundraising capacity over time, adding new donors, broadening the base, and developing and enabling more volunteers to help with fundraising activities.

Partnership with the Donor Community

Assemble a group of executive directors in a room with program officers from large foundations, and very often those executive directors, a group of otherwise strong, opinionated people, become clones of Uriah Heep[1] Executive directors, as well as development and other staff at nonprofits, have mental models of foundations, other philanthropic institutions, and large donors. Likewise, donors and program officers also have mental models of nonprofits and the people who work for them. Money changes everything; people act very strangely around funders, mostly out of unnecessary levels of fear and apparent need. All the players, from givers to middle-people (the nonprofits) and end users, need to remember the concept of *exchange*. Given this concept, no one is begging and *the need is never about money*. Rather, it is about community, people, and mission.

Being authentic, true to yourself, and true to your agency's mission and constituents' needs is the only real path to take with funders. By being an honest window of interpretation on the needs of the community – backed by real data, not just folksy anecdotes, you will gain the ear of donors. By having a cost-effective strategy that makes a difference, you will gain their respect. If your strategies and mission are a match with the donor's philanthropic mission – and you have laid out a sensible, cost-effective plan, you will likely get funded.

Executive directors, development staff, and board members should seek out and promote active partnerships with donors whose philanthropic mission is close to the agency's mission. Increasingly, this work is being made more complex through partnering across the field of work (the arts, social services, community organizations) and the need to find philanthropic partners to help move collaboratives or broad-based initiatives forward. Too often, however, it is the foundation staff, government funders or donors who promote the partnership or collaborative concept first.

[1] Literature note: an ingratiating, smarmy character from Charles Dickens' *David Copperfield*.

Staff and nonprofit boards (who are close to the consumers of donated dollars) need to: (a) bring those end users into fuller partnership with the analysis of need and future programming; and (b) be proactive in providing foundations and other donors with ideas, concepts, and programs that make sense. Relationship-building is about taking risks; those in the nonprofit sector need to take risks with funders and with their constituents, while remaining their authentic selves.

The Small Shop: What It Takes

The majority of nonprofits operate from the small shop model, with one or two people implementing all of the tasks related to fundraising.

If possible, set aside a separate work area for fund development. It does not have to be the best office space in the agency, but it should have the best computer system. Since fundraising relies on building databases and researching information, the system should be equipped with an updated word processing program, spreadsheet program, and database management program. If the development office produces a newsletter and other marketing materials, the computer should also have desktop publishing capabilities.

Success in fundraising depends in part on *maintaining good fundraising records.* Too many nonprofits have lost years of donor names and giving histories when their computers crashed. To avoid losing vital information:

- Always back up donor files.
- Develop companion hard files.
- Organize folders by categories, such as government, foundations, corporations, religious institutions, and individual donors.
- Keep copies of all correspondence and records of gifts.
- Keep the database updated with notes on changes in program staff or donor status.
- Archive older correspondence so that new development staff will have access to old records.

In addition, keep records of feedback and analysis of fundraising appeals so that future staff will have information such as which mail houses have been troublesome, which volunteers are so high-maintenance they should be avoided, which caterers to use, etc. Fund development is hard work, and staff turnover is high, so do your future colleagues a favor and maintain an institutional memory through the written word.

Nonprofit development staff must have access to the Internet since most foundations and government funding applications are now available on line. For startups and agencies that are simply too poor to afford access, set aside time to go to Associated GrantMakers or other libraries to research funding sources over the web.

Sustaining Development and Emerging Trends

Sustainable Programs

Sustainable programs depend upon acquiring new donors and upgrading active donors to larger gifts. Keep good records and maintain regular communication with donors (including thank-you notes and organizational updates). Maintain a sound reputation by offering meaningful, cost-effective programs and working to minimize staff turnover that can create instability.

It is particularly important for boards to minimize turnover of executive directors and for executive directors to minimize turnover of development staff. Board members should ensure thoughtful succession planning at the governance level to ensure a mix of seasoned leaders and new energy.

Sustainable programs depend on fund development plans that call for a broad mix of sources and that challenge the board, staff and fundraising volunteers to do a little bit more each year.

Emerging Trends

New technology will continue to have an impact on philanthropy for years to come, as will the affluence that has been generated through technology. Younger donors, who tend to view themselves as social investors, will give less to pooled general funds and more directly to causes they care about.

Emerging vehicles for funding include charitable remainder trusts, family foundations, and donor-advised funds. Development staff will need to include these vehicles in their research and communicate with the professionals who serve as advisors to the individuals and families who make use of them.

Charitable remainder trusts allow donors to give cash, stock, real estate, or other assets to a charity, which then invests the gift and provides regular payments to the donor, a beneficiary named by the donor, or both. When the donor and any other beneficiaries die, all the assets in the trust go to the charity.

Donor-advised funds are financial accounts from which donors can easily make grants. Contributions to donor-advised funds are irrevocable; donors receive immediate tax advantages and can make donations from either the interest earnings on the account or from the principal and interest earnings. Donor-advised funds are legally controlled by, and exist within, public charities that have been so designated by the IRS. Donor-advised funds are most commonly managed by community foundations, but financial service firms are becoming major players in this arena.

More fundraising vehicles will emerge as the World War II generation makes what will be the largest transfer of wealth to heirs in our nation's history, and as new fortunes continue to be made in emerging technologies.

PUBLIC RELATIONS

We owe a debt of gratitude to Charlotte Ryan of Boston College and Karen Jeffreys of the Rhode Island Coalition Against Domestic Violence, both of whom have built on the work of Annette Duke. Charlotte's teachings and Karen's work have informed our practice to such an extent that this chapter in large part reflects what we have learned from them.

– Third Sector New England

CHAPTER 8

Communication is one of the key competencies of the information age. Nonprofits must plan as strategically for communications needs as they do for fund development – on an annual basis using the strategic plan as a base and employing strategic thinking.

Communications planning defines all of the stakeholders and audiences with whom a nonprofit must communicate. It also includes all of the methods and tools required for that communication to happen. In this chapter, we will provide a guide to strategic communications planning for nonprofit organizations.

Strategic Media Planning

Definitions

Public relations, marketing, media, communications planning. What is the difference?

Public relations is simply relating to your audience – anyone you need to communicate with in order to accomplish your goals and meet your mission. Some public relations people refer to their audience as their "publics." We will use the term "audience" in this guide.

Marketing is somewhat interchangeable with public relations. But it can also refer to the specific packaging of the products offered by the nonprofit to the public. We will use the term *public relations* generally, with the understanding that marketing is incorporated under public relations.

Media refers to broadcast and print outlets such as network television, cable television, newspapers and magazines, radio stations, wire services, and the Internet.

Communications planning includes defining all the stakeholders and audiences with whom a nonprofit needs to communicate and the methods and tools by which that communication happens.

The following table describes various media outlets, the opportunities they present, and the ways that an organization can work with them to get their message out.

Media Outlets and Opportunities

Media Outlets	Services and Methods Provided by Media Outlets	Nonprofit's Role
Television: Network and Cable	Media event attendance	Media advisory Press release
	Breaking news story	Press statement Press release Call to give quote
	Feature story	Call to pitch story Follow-up with information
	Talk show	Call to get on show
	Public service announcements (PSA)	Creation of video or print product
	Paid advertising	Creation or purchase of ad
	Calendar listing (cable only)	Submission or purchase of listing

Media Outlets	Services and Methods Provided by Media Outlets	Nonprofit's Role
Radio	Media event attendance	Media advisory Press release
	Breaking news story	Press statement Press release Call to give quote
	Talk show	Call to get on show
	Public service announcement (PSA)	Creation of tape or print product
	Paid advertising	Creation or purchase of ad
Wire services: AP (Associated Press),UPI (United Press International),and Reuters	Media event attendance	Media advisory Press release
	Breaking news story	Press statement Press release Call to give quote
Newspapers: Daily, Weekly, Monthly	Media event attendance	Media advisory Press release
	News story	Press statement Press release Call to give quote
	Feature story	Call to pitch story Follow-up with information
	Community calendar listing	Submission of listing
	Editorial/guest editorial (op-ed piece)	Call to pitch story
	Letter to the editor	Submission of letter
	Photo	Submission of photo with release
	Print advertising: display ad, certified ad, and advertising insert	Creation or purchase of ad
Magazines	Feature story	Call to pitch
	Calendar listing	Submission of listing
	Letter to the editor	Submission of letter
	Print advertising: display ad, certified ad, and advertising insert	Creation or purchase of ad
Internet	On-line news	Press release by email
	Website	Creation of site
	Link	Exchange of links
	Listserv	Development of listserv Subscription to useful listservs
	Search engines	Optimization of keywords
	Banner advertising	Purchase

Why Do Communications Planning?

Nonprofits must communicate with their key audiences in order to raise funds, run programs, and meet their mission and goals.

It is easy to make the mistake of thinking that public relations is simply producing a newsletter and relating to media. *It involves much more!* Media is an important tool for communication, but it is only one part. In order to succeed at public relations, your organization needs to look beyond simple media and make a long-term communications plan.

Communications planning is about strategically determining who the audiences are and how to reach them in order to further organizational goals.

Determining the Audiences

An organization's specific audiences will vary, depending on its programs and mission. Typically, nonprofit audiences will include:

- internal audiences of board members, staff, and volunteers; and
- external audiences of clients, donors, legislators, other nonprofits, collaborators, policymakers, and the general public.

Media is both a tool for reaching these audiences and an audience of its own.

As you identify the audiences you want to reach, think about how they like to receive information, whether by television or by radio, in the streets or in newspapers. Consider what they watch and listen to, as well as how often and where. When your audience is the media, consider how to present the material in ways that increase interest in your story.

Developing a Communications Plan

A communications plan will help you be clear about the message you want to send, the audience you want to reach, and the tactics and timelines for reaching them. It also will help you evaluate what works and what doesn't. Keep in mind that even if you do not develop a formal communications plan, you still will be communicating – just not as comprehensively and cohesively as you would with a plan.

Communications planning includes both short- and long-term planning.

- *Short-term planning* is for specific activities such as a special event or the kickoff of a new program, initiative, or legislative lobbying effort. In short-term planning, the organization needs to be clear about:
  - its objective;
  - its audience for the event or activity;
  - its message to that audience; and
  - how it will reach that audience.

After implementation, the organization can evaluate the effectiveness of the communications plan.

- *Long-term planning* is for organizations that want to make a strategic plan that furthers the mission of the entire organization, not just a specific activity or event. The *first step* in long-term planning is to define the organization's goals and objectives – which should match those outlined in the annual operations plan or any other plans that exist. For each goal:
  - Define which audiences need to be reached.
  - List all possible tactics and tools that will reach the desired audiences. (See **Beyond Media** later in this chapter.)
  - Define the key message to each audience, recognizing that it may change from one audience to another.
  - Think through how to evaluate success at getting the message out to the desired audiences.

Once you've done this for each of the organization's major goals – voilá – you have a communications plan! Next, assign a person to each tactic and decide on a timeline for completing the task. This step is necessary to help the organization understand that while there are many great ideas, they can't all be implemented. The next step is to prioritize what can be accomplished realistically and set the plan in motion.

Sample Communications Plan

This is a snapshot of what a communications plan looks like. A full plan would include all of the goals, objectives and strategies for your organization. In addition, a goal can contain several objectives, each of which can have more than one strategy and more than one audience.

Goal: **To better serve the needs of domestic violence victims from traditionally under-served communities**

Objective 1: To increase by 5 percent the number of victims from under-served communities who use our services

Strategy: To launch a new initiative aimed at serving victims living in rural areas

Primary audience: Victims living in rural areas (List towns you plan to serve.)

Tactics to reach victims living in rural areas:

- Hold a focus group of current or past survivors to get ideas on outreach.
- Hold a focus group of key stakeholders in the area (police, community organizations, key leaders, etc.) to get ideas on outreach.
- Design and develop a new brochure that explains the program.
- Send out a brochure via direct mail to every household in rural areas.
- Put up informational displays at key areas in the community (library, police department, bank, hair salons, movie theater, churches, etc.).
- Hold individual meetings with key leaders and stakeholders in the town to develop relationships with them.
- Hold meetings with key clergy members in the area to secure their support and involvement.
- Hold a press conference to launch the new initiative.
- Initiate four PSAs to each radio and paper that serves the rural town.
- Initiate two feature stories.
- Arrange to speak on six radio or television talk shows.
- Initiate 25 speaking engagements at churches, schools, and civic and business groups.

Key messages:

- You are not alone; there is help.
- Contact us and we will help you.
- No one deserves to be abused.

Evaluation factors:

- Increase in calls by victims living in rural areas.
- Increase in participation by key stakeholders in the town.

Working with the Media

A media plan goes a step further than a communications plan. The media plan outlines, in detail, how the organization will achieve good media coverage. *Do not* make the mistake of thinking that media attention will simply happen. ***You*** make it happen. Consider this: nonprofits do not blame donors for not contributing to the organization if they have not been asked, but they do tend to blame the media for not covering their issues when they have done nothing to promote them. The days of Lois Lane and Clark Kent are over – if you want your story covered, you need to sell it.

Media work takes planning, just as program delivery and fund development do. Media work involves preparing an annual plan that includes action steps and timelines.

Getting Started

The main purpose of media planning is to make sure that you don't miss deadlines or forget important steps in getting your message out. It does not have to be a time-consuming activity; you or your staff can make the suggested timeline as detailed or brief as will be helpful to the organization in getting its message out in a timely manner. To get started:

1. List all the activities that are planned for the agency over the next 12-month period and that should be promoted through the media. Include in this list any events, activities, public awareness campaigns, and new initiatives that will be launched.
2. Note on a calendar the target date of each item on the list.
3. Note, working backwards on the same calendar, all the known media opportunities and associated tasks related to media coverage of the activity.

On a time line (as below), note months and known opportunities:

- PSA for radio, print, and television (Prepare one month ahead of time – September.)
- Talk shows (Start setting up opportunities in August.)
- Talk show appearances in September and October to promote an event or program.
- Feature stories (Depending on the size of a newspaper, nonprofits need a one- to three-month timeline to identify reporters and pitch the story. Major newspapers, monthlies, and magazines need as much as a four- to six-month lead time.)
- Media advisories and press releases (Send the week of the event to encourage media outlets to cover the event.)
- Photo and press releases (Sent immediately after the event to local papers and magazines.)

After you have noted the known media opportunities, look over the calendar and note where gaps occur. Consider filling them with media opportunities that are not specifically related to the main event, but that will bring attention to the agency. Some examples include:

- press conference to announce a new initiative;
- letter to the editor thanking the community for their support;
- op ed piece to educate the public on programs and services; or
- feature story on any programs or initiatives.

Be timely in choosing your approaches to the media. For instance, pitch a new education-related program in September when the media is focused on the school-year startup.

Example: Annual fundraiser to be held in October

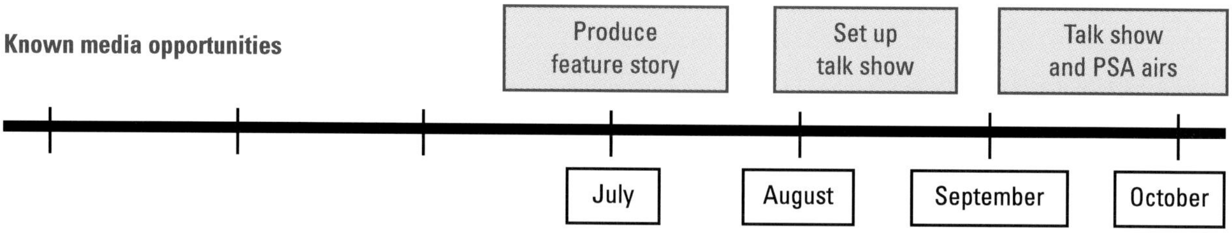

Known media opportunities

	July	August	September	October
Known media opportunities	Produce feature story	Set up talk show		Talk show and PSA airs

Developing Relationships

Developing relationships with people who work at media outlets is essential if you hope to receive good media coverage. Get to know reporters, assignment editors, editors, photographers and camera people, producers, talk show hosts, and PSA directors. If you have public relations staff, they should be developing these relationships as a matter of course. If you, as executive director, are responsible for public relations, take time to think through how to reach the key contacts in the media. *Find out who covers your issue areas for your local media. Ask other nonprofits (that routinely get good coverage) who the good contacts are. Call these contacts. Introduce yourself. Find out the best way to work with them.*

Case Study: Project RIGHT Challenges Local Television News Practices[1]

With advances in satellite technology and increased monopoly ownership of local television networks, local TV newscasts often provide less local coverage in favor of airing material from national affiliates. With notable exceptions, the local stories that do reach the airwaves are often riddled with stereotypes and errors, which suggest unfamiliarity with local neighborhoods and politics.

After a local television station showed footage of the home and family members of a child who had allegedly been sexually assaulted, Project RIGHT, Inc. (Rebuild and Improve Grove Hall Together of Roxbury, MA) decided to challenge the rush to the bottom of the barrel stories that so many local TV news stations currently engage in. With technical assistance and staff support from the Media Research Action Project (MRAP), Project RIGHT began an initiative to study media coverage, specifically of Grove Hall, and then began a dialogue, with local affiliate WHDH-TV (the station that aired the child's name), which quickly expanded to include other local print and broadcast media.

Studies Provide Talking Points

Project RIGHT surveyed almost 200 Grove Hall residents to establish their reactions to media coverage of their neighborhood. Simultaneously, MRAP monitored how local TV news portrayed Roxbury and other Boston communities of color. The survey ascertained that, on average, only 6 percent of local TV news affiliates had any positive civic coverage-any stories that covered politics, business, the environment, education, housing, and youth (with the exception of crime or accident stories involving youth). In contrast, more than half of the stories that aired rehashed the details of accidents and crimes, providing little context by which to assess those incidents.

This study resulted in the Building Bridges conference, co-sponsored by Project RIGHT, the Boston Association of Black Journalists (BABJ), WHDH-TV, and other media outlets. Held in late November 1998, the conference was well attended by both media and area nonprofits. Although conference presenters discussed negative media coverage of Roxbury and other communities of color, the tone of the conference was collaborative. Project RIGHT invited local media to experiment together to strengthen news coverage of Roxbury and Boston's other communities of color. The media outlets responded by committing to ongoing dialogues with community-based organizations; since then they have covered a number of wider-ranging stories about environmental problems in Roxbury and land development issues.

The conference represented a breakthrough, explains Jorge Martinez, Project RIGHT's director: "We work on many neighborhood and community issues, as well as citywide issues that relate to violence prevention and quality of life. Because the media helps the general public form perspectives on issues like traffic, safety, violence against the elderly, domestic violence, and city services, it's important we get our perspective in the mix. Media exposure helps us to be efficient and effective in addressing emergencies and building support for change in public policy. We also connect with others who are interested in similar issues."

[1] Reprinted from the Nonprofit Quarterly, Spring 1999.

Understanding the Goal

The goal of media work is twofold:

1. getting the media's attention; and
2. working with the media to get a clear message across to your audience.

Pitching the Story

To pitch a story, you must be able, within the first 30 seconds, to tell a reporter why the story is newsworthy. And you must have the *who, what, when, where, and how* prepared and laid out ahead of time. The reporter may not always be interested in your story, but if he or she is, you must have all the pieces of the story ready.

Think like a reporter. Develop the beginning, middle, and end of the story you want to pitch. Make your case for why it is newsworthy. Most small, local papers are looking for stories, so if you develop sound, newsworthy stories and keep pitching them to reporters you have developed relationships with, your agency will get coverage.

For example, suppose your organization is launching a new program that you believe is newsworthy because it meets a new and different need in the community. One option is to call a press conference to announce the program – hopefully bringing the reporters to you. Another option is to call individual reporters. If there is interest, you can send background material and connect the reporter with people who can be interviewed according to his or her own schedule.

Framing the Message

Framing is the process of ordering the facts and pieces of the story in such a way that the message you want to get across is made clear. No story is completely neutral; all stories have a "spin" or perspective. In order for your message to be as meaningful as possible to the audience you most want to reach, you need to "frame the story" so that the most important facts and points of view lead the coverage. *Framing should not be left to reporters.* The emphasis and perspective that you care about may get lost if you do not create the "spin" yourself.

The "Media Caucus" as a Tool for Framing Messages

A "media caucus" can be used for framing messages by bringing together a subset of co-workers to develop a message to the media. Sit down with a group of people, including the spokesperson for the project and other staff knowledgeable about the story you will be pitching and ask the following questions:

- What is the hook for the press?
- Who is our audience?
- What is our key message?
- What are the key talking points?
- What are good sound bites to use?
- What might the media ask us and what will our response be?

To improve your ability to interact with the media and learn more about what they might ask, take notes each time you are interviewed or have someone taking notes during a face-to-face interview.

Sometimes the media will seek you out to get a quote or background information on a burning issue. Use the opportunity to be proactive and frame the message. When a reporter calls, ask:

- if there is a deadline;
- what the reporter's angle is; and
- what the reporter wants from you or your organization.

Use the responses to gather the reporter's assumptions about the story, your organization, and its response to the story. This information will inform your "emergency media caucus." After gathering the information, tell the reporter you will call back within the parameters of the deadline – whether that means calling back within five minutes or 24 hours.

The ultimate purpose of the media caucus – whether routine or emergency – is to allow the spokesperson or person being interviewed to practice. Role-play the questions the group has come up with, and let the spokesperson practice the responses the group has developed. Even if you feel silly, do the role-play. Comfort with the material and interview setting comes with practice; even the most experienced speakers take time to think through and run through what they want to say.

Beyond Media

While media is very important, keep in mind that there are other ways to reach your audiences. Other public relations tools include:

- telephone calls;
- e-mail;
- internet websites;
- letters;
- faxes;
- flyers;
- leaflets;
- fact sheets;
- studies and reports;
- videos;
- newsletters;
- events;
- brochures and other agency materials;
- faith community bulletins;
- meetings;
- posters; and
- trainings.

Public awareness tools and materials also include:

- billboards;
- bus advertisements;
- radio, television, and printed PSAs;
- ads, posters, point-of-purchase displays, and palm cards; and
- press conferences, political actions, and community and fundraising events.

The benefit of these public relations tools is that they allow the organization to have control over the message; each can be used to reach a specific audience. Developing a communications plan will help you determine your key audiences and the best tactics for reaching them.

Public Relations Systems

The following systems can help you ensure that sound public relations practices and media work.

- *Develop a press list* and keep it in your database. This is your list of contacts and means of reaching them at various media outlets. Keep it updated.
- *Develop a media protocol* that describes the chain of command of spokespersons for your agency. A call from the media should always go to a person, not that person's voice mail. Make sure your media protocol indicates who should take an initial call.
- *Develop a clip book* of print articles about your organization. You can hire a clipping service for this purpose, or ask board members or volunteers to clip every article they see that mentions the organization.
- *Develop media forms* to record information about on-air and print interviews so that key speaking points are recorded for later use. Include the locations, names of staff, and directions to stations.
- *Develop a fax or e-mail system* so that you can send press releases, media advisories, pitch letters, and PSAs to media outlets automatically.

Final Tips

- Don't be overwhelmed by media or public relations. Assess where you are currently, and take some small steps at first. If you currently get no coverage, make a goal to get one newspaper article in the next year.
- Remember that good communication is not magic. It happens because the organization makes it a priority and devotes energy, time, and resources to it. Since most organizations do not have the resources for even a part-time public relations staff person, the executive director must assume this responsibility or make sure that it is delegated to other staff. Be disciplined about devoting time – even one hour a week – to public relations planning and implementation.
- Don't spend money on agency materials that have not been developed with a particular audience and message in mind. Always plan before taking action.

Glossary of Media Terms

Events

News Conference: An event staged exclusively for the press where one or more people, but no more than four, read prepared statements and answer reporters' queries. A news conference should be called only if there is something timely and extremely important to announce. Simply announcing that October is Domestic Violence Awareness Month most likely will not draw reporters to a news conference, but having the mayor present to read a proclamation and speak to a new community effort might create interest.

Press Briefing: An informal, by-invitation-only meeting at which advocates give reporters background and information. Press briefings often take place over breakfast and usually involve one to three presenters and up to 12 reporters. Briefings are held to bring reporters up to speed on facts relating to an incident or a report that might be important to the program and the community. Fact sheets and other background materials should be distributed. Domestic Violence Awareness Month might be a good opportunity to educate key reporters in your area about the pervasiveness of domestic violence in your city and nationwide.

Press Opportunity: An event that is not planned for the media but which reporters may attend. Rallies, marches, candlelight vigils, fundraisers, public speeches or appearances, awards ceremonies, and issue forums are press opportunities.

Photo Opportunity: A press opportunity that has a particularly good visual component that is worthy of space in a newspaper or magazine.

Pre-interview: A telephone conversation with a producer of a talk show. Pre-interviews are used to make certain that the prospective guest is intelligent, articulate, well-versed on the issue, quick on his or her feet, and interesting to listen to. A pre-interview requires the same serious preparation as the interview itself.

Materials

Media Advisory: A one-page dated announcement of an upcoming event such as a press or photo opportunity. A media advisory should include a contact name and telephone number so that reporters can call for further information. It is sent to the assignment editors, reporters, editors, and producers on your press list.

News Release: A two- to four-page report of a newsworthy event. A news release should be written as an article because outlets will print portions of good news releases often appear in print verbatim. A news release must include: a contact to call for further information, a first sentence that grabs the reader, a quote from a spokesperson or agency leader, and additional background information. A news release would be issued in conjunction with the activities held for Domestic Violence Awareness Month and would be distributed at the time of the events – by mail, fax or distribution by hand.

Backgrounder: An in-depth explanation that can be used to help a reporter who is completely new to an issue become familiar with it.

Fact Sheet: A one-page information sheet that often contains statistics or other data.

Statement: A brief – one page, maximum – commentary with the prepared remarks of a spokesperson. A statement should be dated and should include a contact name and telephone number. If you hold a news conference, a rally or other public event, you will want to issue statements that all the speakers can distribute to the press. A statement can also be used to respond quickly to a breaking story, such as a highly publicized incident of abuse. It must be prepared and distributed within an hour or two of an event, and must be quotable. Good reporters often follow up a statement with questions, but having a statement helps the reporter insert commentary into the story immediately. It also increases the likelihood that the exact message you want relayed is the one the reporter uses.

Press Kit: A packet of information, usually in a pocket folder, that is distributed to the media at news conferences, at press briefings, or in response to requests for information. A press kit may contain news releases, statements, background fact sheets, and materials such as newsletters and brochures that are not designed specifically for the media.

Calendar Notice: A short, one-page notification of events that are of interest to the public. A calendar notice or announcement is intended to air or to be published.

Pitch Letters: A personalized note that specifically urges a particular reporter to cover an event or issue. Such a letter often describes a particularly newsworthy aspect of an event.

Edit Memo: A short memorandum, addressed to editorial page editors or members of an editorial board, asking them to devote space to an issue. A good editorial memo contains several well-written paragraphs that can be lifted and used in an editorial. Use an edit memo to direct editorial writers to specific issues. It's a good idea to include suggestions for actions that people can take.

Op-ed Piece: A 500- to 700-word signed guest editorial that is submitted to newspapers for the editorial page. An op-ed piece should emphasize the writer's opinion or experience and should be of interest to the general public.

Letter to the Editor: A letter from a newspaper reader that responds to reports or editorials with a confirming or opposing point of view and that often expands on a point made in the original article. A letter to the editor should be brief, to the point, and signed by the program director, an affected party, or another representative.

PSA: A public service announcement or public service spot is a brief announcement made on behalf of a nonprofit organization on both radio and television. Like a commercial, it is limited to a specific length, must be non-political, and should be of wide interest and benefit to the public.

COMMUNITY DEVELOPMENT AND GOVERNMENT RELATIONS

CHAPTER 9

In this chapter, we address community development and government relations together, to emphasize that both are concerned primarily with relationship-building. The goal of community development[1] is to *bring members of a community together to identify and combat shared problems in a way that includes those members in making decisions that affect their lives and allows them to develop long-term capacity for problem-solving.* Government relations brings people together to *identify shared problems and to educate, inform and sometimes lobby government officials* – legislative and administrative – *toward bringing about change in the policies and practices that affect people.* Both build toward their goals one step – often one individual – at a time.

In this chapter, we describe how to create a community development effort, define types of community, reflect on the issues involved in working with communities, and discuss goal-setting, participatory practices, the nuts and bolts of organizing, and government relations.

The key thing to remember is that change happens incrementally. There are very few shortcuts to effective community development, but rest assured that every relationship you develop builds a stronger foundation for future change.

Community Development

Community development, at its most basic, involves building the relationships that an organization needs to survive and flourish. *Ongoing community development is a nonprofit's reason for being.* Unless yours is the rare organization – and we've never actually heard of one – that has no need for interaction with the public, your constituents, other stakeholders, or the government, community development is essential for your success and survival.

Creating a Plan

To create a plan, begin by analyzing the strengths and weaknesses of your organization and by considering its opportunities and potential threats. This is sometimes called a SWOT (strengths, weaknesses, opportunities, threats) analysis. Know your staff, your board, and their backgrounds:

- Are they well connected in the community?
- Are you willing to spread community development work out among the staff?
- Are you relying on the same people all the time?
- Are there holes in your process?
- Are there communities within your community that you are failing to address?

Before you can answer these questions, you need to be clear about who and where your community is and what your community development goals are.

Elements of Community Development

The best community development work does not follow an orderly, step-by-step formula. People and issues will evolve and actions will build from other actions. All of the following elements need attention in varying degrees throughout the process.

1. *Think BIG or go home.* This organizing expression is an appropriate one with which to begin any community development discussion. It means that you should start your process by thinking as big as you can, by first considering what the ideal outcome to your effort would be, and then by working from there.
2. Define your community. Ask yourself and your staff:
   - Who are we trying to reach?
   - Who are we trying to involve?
   - Who wants or is in need of our support?
3. Define the problem – a clear goal depends on a firm community base. If the community isn't clear about what it wants, it will be less effective.
4. Assess the strengths and weaknesses in the ability of people within a community to effect change.

[1] Of great help to us in collecting our thoughts about community development was the work of Herbert J. Rubin and Irene S. Rubin of Northern Illinois University. Their book, *Community Organizing and Development* (Needham Heights, MA: Allyn and Bacon, 1992) is a good basic text on the subject.

5 Assess the competencies of the staff and volunteers to provide leadership and support in an inclusive, participatory manner.

6 Provide training and support for staff, volunteers, and community leaders.

7 Develop ground rules for recruitment of, and participation by, community members.

8 Conduct outreach (See Chapter 8, **Public Relations**.)

a. Make a list of community leaders who should be made aware of your program and call or write to each one to advise them of your current effort. If possible, follow up with a visit. Challenge yourself to reach out to people who might not be obvious supporters. Include in your list:

- ministers;
- politicians; and
- parent/teacher associations.

b. Canvass the neighborhood through door-to-door contacts, flyers, and posters in key locations such as:

- laundromats;
- clinics;
- churches;
- attorneys' offices; and
- other places your potential clients may frequent.

c. Create telephone trees (with each person responsible for calling three to five others, who then call three to five others, etc.) and other systems of personal contact to advise and update community members of new projects and issues.

9 Keep in touch. Once contact has been established with community leaders, stay in touch through periodic telephone calls, notes, e-mails, newsletters, or updates. Create a routine advisory system using e-mail, fax, regular mail, newsletters, or telephone calls to keep active participants and community members informed of, and involved in, your actions.

10 Make links to other organizations through any means possible. Cooperate on collective events with like-minded organizations:

- Form coalitions of supportive organizations so you can solicit each other's members and activists when more people power is needed.
- Create formal networks, associations, and alliances.
- Collaborate on joint actions.

Defining Your Community

Community development begins by defining the community in need of development. The community may be based on geographic proximity, common heritage, social class or condition in life, interest in an issue, or ideology. The important thing is that the members must see themselves as a community – or at least see the potential for becoming one. The type of community you serve will often determine the kind of work to be done. A physically cohesive community will likely require different organizing techniques than a community that is based on a common interest but whose members circle the globe. Your organization needs to *be very clear about who its community is.*

In addition, your organization needs to *be very clear about how it wants to work with that community.* Community development organizations include:

- social equity organizations that work to provide their members with individual benefits such as welfare payments, subsidized rent, school vouchers, or social security benefits;
- self-help organizations that help people come together to help themselves form support groups or cooperatives for food, housing, or health;
- community identity organizations that work to instill pride and cohesiveness and can be mobilized in the future for specific action; and
- social justice organizations that work on broad issues such as cleaning the environment, supporting human rights, or changing public sentiment about safety issues such as drinking and driving.

The following list defines various types of communities and reflects on some of the issues faced in developing them.

- A community based on *geographic proximity* is one where community members all reside or work within a geographically defined area such as a city, town, or neighborhood.
    - Community identity tends to be fairly strong, although the level of commitment members demonstrate for getting involved depends on their investment and attachment – physical, financial, and/or emotional – in the community.
    - Efforts to activate members of the community will be affected by the clarity of solutions to common problems. Members of a geographic community are likely to rally around issues such as airport noise, recycling needs, deteriorating housing stock, and safety because it is relatively easy to choose an appropriate action and determine who is responsible for making change – a city councilor, state legislator, or park board representative.
    - Residents are easier to mobilize when action is systematic. Building a playground in a local park can be broken down into clear steps that individual community members can choose to become active in: locating appropriate land; finding businesses or individuals to donate material or equipment; writing grants; organizing a work day or two; publicizing the event; or hosting it.
    - It is relatively easy to contact people and to get them to come together. Traditional methods of contact include local newspapers and newsletters; door-to-door canvassing; and flyers in neighborhood hang-outs, shops, schools and churches.
    - The benefits of working together are very clear. Whether or not a specific action has been successful, individual connections will have been made, setting the stage for future work and creating a feeling of neighborliness among residents who got to know each other.
- Communities of *common heritage* may be based in a specific location or may have members from across many geographic regions. Communities based on common heritage include communities of people of the same race, ethnic heritage, religious belief, or national origin.
    - Identification with the community tends to be very strong, although commitment to the community will vary greatly depending on the degree to which individual members identify *primarily* with the community of common heritage.
    - Efforts to activate the membership will be affected by the urgency of purpose of the organizing effort. Members of an association based on ethnic heritage who enjoy receiving a regular newsletter and occasionally showing up at a social event may become active in soliciting funds and collecting clothing for a drive based on renewed problems in their country of origin. When the strife is over, they may retreat to their former, less-involved status.
    - Members are easiest to mobilize when they see a clear need for their involvement or a personal benefit to closer association.
    - It is somewhat more difficult to reach potential members of associations based on common heritage. If the community exists within a common geographic location, many of the traditional outreach tactics will work well. If the community is more dispersed, outreach methods may include community newspapers and newsletters, feature stories that reflect timely action, church bulletins, word of mouth, and the Internet.
    - The benefits of working together tend to be less obvious in an economic or social justice sense, but include pride, a feeling of belonging, and an ability to be helpful beyond what is possible on an individual basis.
- Communities of *social class or condition in life* may include workers at a plant, workers in an industry, or those who are professionally associated.
    - Community identity tends to be strong, but the level of commitment is usually very specifically based on economics.
    - Efforts to activate members will depend on specific strategies that have the potential to

directly or indirectly enhance the member's economic well-being. Labor union affiliation increases when members believe the union gets results; professional organizations thrive when members see a professional benefit from socializing, learning, or serving greater society with their peers.

- Members mobilize beyond their own self-interest when they see that they have issues in common with others, when they are able to act as role models for others, and when lack of involvement will isolate them from their peers.
- Outreach within social class communities is relatively straightforward and can be accomplished through posters and flyers in the workplace, direct mail to license holders, professional journals, newsletters, payroll inserts, word of mouth, and general interest news articles that alert people to the organization.
- The economic and professional growth benefits of working together are fairly easy to see. Other benefits may be more intangible but include social inclusion, intellectual growth, and an ability to indirectly promote social change.

- Communities based on *interest in an issue or ideology* draw members from within specific localities as well as diverse geographic regions. Communities based on ideology may focus on such issues as promoting social justice, health, housing, safety, education, or partisan beliefs.
  - Community identity based on ideology or interest in an issue tends to be fairly weak for most members. Commitment will depend on the level of passion an individual member has for the issue, but keep in mind that rarely is the cause in question of primary importance to community members.
  - Efforts to activate members will depend on the relevance of the cause to the daily life of the members and the specificity of the action, combined with the level of involvement that is requested.
  - Members mobilize most readily when they are able to be part of a larger action with little individual effort, when a cause is particularly relevant, and when the groundwork has been laid to such an extent that it is becoming clear that the issue has social relevance. Organizing to promote legislation against drunk drivers, for example, is easier to accomplish now that a core group of mothers has brought the issue to social prominence and proved that change can be forced with hard work from a relatively small group and minimal action from large numbers of people.
  - Outreach around issues and ideology is less straightforward than for other types of communities. Potential members can be widespread and not socially cohesive. Many potential members will not see that they have enough in common with others who share their beliefs to make it necessary to come together in community. Using the mass media to promote the issue and bring public awareness that an organization exists to work on it is a valuable approach. Other methods of outreach include direct mail through shared lists of similar organizations, the Internet, and word of mouth.
  - The benefits of working together are often intangible. Social change can be slow to accomplish. Pride in supporting a good cause, getting to know like-minded people, and the ability to throw oneself into creating social change are all benefits of belonging to a community based on ideology.

Setting Your Goals

Your community development goals will change with time and conditions.

- If your organization is new, your goal may be to find members who will consider themselves part of your community.
- If your organization is a neighborhood agency, you might already have a good sense of who your members are but need to find a way to let them come together and set the agenda.

- If you are new to organizing, your goal might be to increase the number of participants in any action you are planning.
- If you have been around for awhile, your goal might be to work yourself out of a job by empowering community members to do the work.

The key thing is to make sure that the process you undertake truly does enable members of the community to play a substantial role in setting goals and working toward meeting them.

The *main purpose of community development should be to encourage and allow community members to take control of the agenda.* Power will be built slowly, step by step – sometimes, tiny step by tiny step. So, in order to avoid getting sidetracked along the way or burnt out because you haven't achieved your end goal, it is important to formulate intermediate goals. Intermediate goals can range from specific to general, as long as they are meaningful, relevant, and helpful in sustaining the organization for the long haul. Some examples of intermediate goals include the following:

- Create a link between individuals and larger, more formidable institutions, helping people gain power within, and recognition by, these institutions by aggregating individual concerns into a sizeable force.
- Promote democracy by helping people become informed on this issue so that they can participate effectively in the public debate.
- Teach people how to sustain meaningful conflict and negotiate from strength.
- Be responsive to community members when taking a leadership role.
- Create a sense of community.
- Contribute to the common good of the broader society by promoting an issue.
- Improve the quality of life of individual members through the resolution of a common problem.
- Reduce the level of inequities in the treatment of people with this condition.
- Help people exercise their constitutional rights.
- Preserve democratic principles.
- Enable people to achieve their potential.
- Have professional organizers work themselves out of a job because community members have developed their own skills and created the resources needed for a sustained effort.

In setting organizational goals – we can't say it strongly enough – keep in mind that your goal is to encourage participation and to build expertise. It is *not* to force everyone to do the same thing at the same time or to adhere to a schedule *you* have devised. So, don't expect everyone to join – you'll only be disappointed if you do. Allow different levels of involvement according to the commitment and energy demonstrated and achievable by community members. Understand that people who are already involved in something are likely to get involved in something else. And, remember that people who identify with a community and feel or express some dissatisfaction will be most likely to become active in developing it.

Participatory Practices

Your own commitment to participatory practices will go a long way toward achieving them within your organization. Continually ask yourself:

- Who is making the decisions?
- Who is speaking out?
- Are people learning new skills that will allow them to hold their own in a larger group?
- Will the skills they are learning be effective beyond the immediate project?

Make participatory practices an independent element and a fundamental dynamic of your organization's community development efforts. Emphasize the *process* of community participation as well as the *goal* of community participation. Think strategically about how to *create and sustain* active participation:

- Plan your approach for promoting participation.
- Allow enough time. Meaningful participation takes time. The process of participation must unfold in rhythm with the natural pace of the people involved or they will never take ownership of the process.

- Set the right tone from the start. An initial meeting where only the "leadership" makes presentations may reveal your true intentions.
- Use a team approach. If commitment to participatory practices doesn't exist throughout the organization, your effort won't be as effective as it could be.

We can't really talk meaningfully about community participation in development if the forces that have caused their exclusion in the past are not confronted from the outset. Recognize that people often feel helpless; fear and feelings of helplessness can stand in the way of developing your community, so understand what's at play and respect it. Be aware that many disenfranchised people believe:

- Problems are too complex and require knowledge they lack.
- They are to blame – even for problems they didn't cause.
- They will face retaliation if they get involved.
- Those in authority must be right.
- They wouldn't know how to protest even if they wanted to.
- They are dependent on a system that is harming them.

In addition, many people who might be interested in becoming involved in community organizing and would make good activists live in such isolation from other segments of society that they are not even aware of the possibilities open to them. Whether this isolation is a result of geography or social distinctions, it is essential to break down barriers and help people see the potential for change.

You don't want to start the process with a plan for every step and decision, but you may need to take the lead in the early stages of engagement. Leaders need to remember that they are working to mobilize people to find their own strength. *Things will go wrong.* Find the balance between doing it yourself so that you are sure it gets done and creating enthusiasm for participation so that new leaders can develop from within the community. *You can't make every decision,* even if it is clear to you what needs to take place. Unless you can involve others in your belief, your efforts won't be as effective and may fail entirely.

Know your community. If local concerns don't mesh with the national concerns of a parent organization, help find a way to emphasize local concerns.
Stay focused. One organization cannot solve every social ill. Issues that you care deeply about may have to be left off the table if they will cause dissension and strife among the membership. If your organization is considering becoming involved in new issues, be prepared for fallout among some of the current members.

Balance mass participation with effective participation. Large-scale involvement is a success only if the participants feel a sense of ownership over the effort. Too many organizations are known only for their leader; make sure that media opportunities and public actions are spread among the membership so they feel, and the organization has made the case, that they have been empowered and not simply manipulated.

Maintain some structure. Participation, especially among larger organizations, can't happen effectively when chaos reigns. Chaotic organizations are susceptible to manipulation by a forceful person.

Act internally as you are asking others to treat you externally. Develop checks and balances within the organization to make sure that people are treated and are treating others fairly and are remaining open to new participants.

Hold successful meetings. The key to a successful meeting is to *have a clear reason for meeting.* Know what must be accomplished by the end of the meeting – not what the decision will be, but *what must be decided.*

- *Have a clear agenda.* Suggested times for discussion help frame the discussion. This can be a subtle guide; topics given 10 minutes for discussion are going to be considered relatively easy to resolve compared to those given 45 minutes.
- *Use a neutral location that is easy to find* and comfortably fits the number of attendees. The room should look full and the participants should appear to be on equal footing; perhaps people with opposing views could sit side by side.

- *Provide refreshments,* if possible.
- *Make sure the sound system is adequate.* Doing what you can to make the physical space comfortable goes a long way toward making participants happy and willing to get involved.
- *Think hard about how to reach your audience* whether with signs, posters, door-to-door flyers, ads in newspapers, circulars, newsletters, or telephone chains. (See Chapter 8, **Public Relations**.) Don't have people leave your planning meeting wondering how organizers who can't organize a meeting are going to plan a large-scale event.

Nuts and Bolts of Organizing, or "Pithy Thoughts to Guide Your Thinking"

- Power is the ability to affect decisions that shape social outcomes.
- Make sure your organization can support the strategies and actions it chooses to promote, or break them into manageable pieces.
- Grow the effort slowly if that is all the organization can handle with the staff and volunteers available. Volunteers can be great, but they take staff time; if you don't have the ability to use volunteers, proceed slowly to develop it.
- You can't develop your organization if you won't give up some control.
- The community development function of an organization cannot be static. Bring in experts to help the staff and leaders learn new skills.
- Build advisory boards. They can be valuable assets in building your community by expanding the eyes and ears you have out in the field, spotting issues and trends, and opening doors for you. An advisory board can meet as a full board or one-on-one, as frequently or infrequently as needed.
- Put your organization in the minds of leaders in your community. Make a list of who's who in your community and take time to introduce your program to them.
- Join state and local community development associations and Internet newsgroups and list-servs to keep abreast of what's new in the field and to meet potential allies.
- Join local organizations that draw community leaders (like the Chamber of Commerce), and go to the meetings, even if you think you don't have the time.
- Do not change the name of your organization unless it is absolutely necessary; it can takes years to make up for lost name recognition.
- Make it easy for people to contact you. Conduct an informal survey; when community members call, ask them how they found you.
- Make sure the person who answers the telephone is pleasant and helpful. Make people *want* to call you, not feel like they are bothering you.
- Talk to all the elected officials and staff who represent your area or specialize in your field so that they know what services you offer and how to refer constituents to you.
- Do not get defensive over lack of knowledge in an area. Listen to advice, ask questions, and don't get upset. Keep in mind that constructive criticism can help you grow to a new level.
- Value people's time. People want to participate when it will help them get to their goals without wasting their time on inefficiencies that have no value. Prepare for meetings by considering the perspective of the person you are meeting with – why and what would they want to know about your and your organization?
- Don't over-promise what you can deliver.
- Be afraid sometimes; if you never are, you aren't reaching far enough.

Government Relations

Government relations involve informing, educating, and sometimes lobbying government officials, both legislative and administrative, about change in the policies and practices that affect people. Contrary to the belief of many in the nonprofit sector, lobbying is not prohibited; it *is* regulated, however, by federal and, often, state law. In this section, we highlight the general guidelines within which your organization must operate, but if your organization spends a significant portion of its resources influencing the *legislative* process or if you have specific questions about your practices or expenditures, we recommend that you seek further information[2] or legal counsel.

Getting Started

Lobbying, in the general sense, means working with elected officials to convince them to take action on an issue within the legislative process. The thought of doing so can seem terribly serious and even frightening to people who are new to the process. Keep in mind, however, that dealing with elected officials and their staff is not much different from dealing with other community leaders. It simply means introducing yourself and your organization to them, getting to know them and their interests, providing information to educate them and support your point of view, and helping them see why they have an interest in working with you to effect change.

Lobbying can take place at any level of government, including town board, city council, school board or committee, county board, state legislature, or U.S. Congress. Since local laws regulating lobbyists may vary, we suggest contacting your city clerk, county administrator, or secretary of state to learn whether local laws apply to you.

General Restrictions

General provisions of tax law that apply to 501(c)3 organizations state that "no substantial part" of their activities may be that of trying to influence legislation. The vagueness of the term "substantial" gives considerable leeway to nonprofit organizations in determining the extent of their involvement in government relations. Many nonprofit organizations, however, that regularly participate in the legislative process have found greater clarity and peace of mind by electing to be covered by "the section 501(h) expenditure test." This 1976 law, and its final regulations, which were issued in 1990, simplified and liberalized the rules for lobbying by nonprofit organizations. The law defines two kinds of lobbying:

- *Direct lobbying* includes communicating directly with legislators and government officials about a specific piece of legislation, or communicating directly with members of your organization to get them to contact legislators about a specific piece of legislation.
- *Grassroots lobbying* is attempting to influence specific legislation by swaying the opinion of the general public. Grassroots lobbying is restricted to one-fourth of the total allowed for lobbying expenditures.

Section 501(h) is concerned with *expenditures* for lobbying, not unreimbursed volunteer efforts. Keep track of your expenditures for lobbying and lobbying-related actions. The law places a ceiling on total expenditures for lobbying according to a formula that begins with 20 percent of the first $500,000 of the organization's budget and ends with 5 percent of the budget over $1.5 million, with a total expenditure cap of $1 million. Not all contacts concerning legislation are considered lobbying that must be included in the expenditure ceiling. Notable exclusions include:

- nonpartisan analysis, study, or research that presents all sides of an issue;
- responses to written requests for assistance from committees or other legislative bodies;
- challenges to, or support for, legislative proposals that would change the organization's rights or right to exist; and
- discussion of broad social or economic policy that may require legislative action as long as the discussion does not address a specific piece of legislation.

Working within the Legislative Process

One of the first decisions you will have to make is whether you, a staff person, a volunteer, or a paid lobbyist will provide direction for the organization's legislative activities. The size of your organization and its level of involvement in the process should be factors in making that decision. Small organizations can usually get along with volunteer lobbyists as long as they have access to enough information to stay abreast of legislative activities, usually through

[2]Excellent sources of information include "The Nonprofit Lobbying Guide" produced by the Independent Sector, *(www.independentsector.org/clpi/index.html), Being a Player, A Guide to IRS Lobbying Regulations for Advocacy Charities* and *Worry-Free Lobbying for Nonprofits,* which are both published by the Alliance for Justice *(www.afj.org).*

alerts put out by a state association. Large organizations will often have paid staff members who serve as the organization's lobbyists as part of their jobs. A middle-ground solution is to hire – either on your own or in association with similar organizations – a "contract" lobbyist who works full-time with several clients. A contract lobbyist will keep an eye on issues relating to your organization and help you to be as effective as possible by letting you know when hearings will take place, informing you of legislation that concerns you, helping you figure out who the key players are, setting up meetings with them, and giving you a link to the interests of similar organizations.

Lobbyists (whether paid or volunteer) should be knowledgeable about the legislative process, familiar with the players, able to get along well with people, and a quick study when it comes to learning about your issues.

How a Bill Becomes a Law

The process in every state is a little different, and it is worth taking the time to understand how an idea becomes a piece of legislation and is brought before a legislative body for consideration. Almost anyone can present an idea to a legislator, city councilor, mayor, or other elected official. In some states, including Massachusetts, any citizen can have a bill introduced for a hearing. In most states, an elected official will meet with a staff attorney who will take the idea, draft it in appropriate legal language, and return it to the legislator who requested it. The proposed legislation will be introduced in the appropriate legislative body, where it will be referred to the committee that deals with its subject matter. The committee's chair will decide if and when it will get a public hearing (usually in consultation with the author of the proposal). The committee will decide at the hearing whether to pass the proposal to the full legislative body. At the local level, the full council or board will take action. At the state and federal level, each body will have to take action. If both pass the proposal, but with different language, the proposal is sent to conference committee, where the differences are worked out.

In tracking any proposal through the process, it is important to find out:

- who is authoring the legislation;
- who else is interested in the subject matter;
- which committees are involved;
- who is chairing the committees that will hear the bill;
- who serves on the committees that hear the bill;
- who represents the district your organization is located in; and
- who the caucus leaders are who control the pace of the process.

Approaching Policy Makers

Begin by figuring out whether connections to the legislature already exist within your organization. Have you or members of your staff, board, or other stakeholders worked on a campaign; made a political contribution; or have friends, colleagues, or family members who serve or work in the legislature? If your community development process is well underway, you may already have been in touch with your local legislators to introduce yourself and your organization.

Elected officials like to know as many of their constituents as possible. They also want to know as much about their district as possible. So, start your government relations effort by contacting your local legislators. Call them up or send them a letter (followed by a telephone call – personal contact is important) and let them know who you are, what your organization does, and why it might be helpful for them to know about you. Let them know if you provide services they might need to refer constituents to, if you will be working on a committee that will be covering legislative issues that year, or if you have a special interest coming up that you would like him or her to be knowledgeable about.

Get to know their staff. Let them know that they can count on you for good information, people to testify at hearings, audiences at public forums, meetings with other legislators and staff, and to help with negotiations, if necessary.

Find out which committees your legislator serves on – most states have a legislative information office which makes such information readily accessible in print or electronic form. Ask your legislator to suggest other members of the legislature who might be especially valuable for you to know. Call them. If they are too busy to see you (which is often the case, especially if you are not from their district), try working with their staff person.

Presenting Information

Always provide solid information. Remember the legislative maxim that "your word is all you have." If you are found to have exaggerated or lied, you may never be trusted again. Stick to the facts. Tell stories with a personal touch whenever possible, but make sure the facts are accurate. Your cause will not be well served if a legislator uses your example in a hearing only to have the media check out the story and find it didn't happen quite that way.

Keep it simple and concise. Most legislators are overwhelmed with reading material. Prepare an executive summary and make sure the full report gets to the staff. Most arguments can be summed up in three to five paragraphs or presented and discussed in under 15 minutes. Don't be disappointed or feel slighted if you can't get an hour with your legislators – their own staff rarely gets to see them for that long.

Keep them advised. If you are presenting information at a hearing, even to a committee that your own legislators don't serve on, make sure you let their office know ahead of time. Legislators like to know when their constituents appear in the capital and will often make a special appearance to show their support.

Compromise Is Not a Dirty Word

Recognize that there are at least two sides to every issue; even your friends won't always be on your side. When dealing with legislators, try to see the argument from their perspective as well as your own. It is usually in the best interest of your organization not to paint legislators into a corner. This does not mean, however, that you should roll over when legislators raise objections. The best lobbyists are able to keep stating and building support for their cause, even as they try to accommodate legitimate concerns. Recognize that there is usually more than one satisfactory solution; help them find a win-win approach.

If a legislator can't or won't support action that gives you everything you want, help find a middle ground that allows you to build on your partial success in the future and keeps the legislator on your side. Remember that today's ogre could be tomorrow's deciding vote.

Find out why a legislator doesn't support your position, and then decide whether to accept, reject, or work with his or her objections. Sometimes the reasons are strictly political – if he or she spent the past year raging over the high costs of recycling, this probably isn't a good year to ask him or her to support funding for a new recycling center in your community. Sometimes the reasons are pragmatic – does he or she object to a funding request because it is not a budget year and his or her colleagues would find it difficult to support at this time? If it's not an emergency, perhaps you can use this year to lay the groundwork and get support for funding next year.

Realize that legislators *can* be persuaded to change their minds; be prepared with solid information, stay in the game, and work with their staff.

Public Hearings

Make your case firmly and concisely. Don't be repetitious and don't go over the time allotted. If several people are presenting for your side, hit the high points and make a slightly different point. If possible, have clients tell their story. Pay attention to the audience; if you are losing them, cut it short. Use appropriate behavior. A public hearing is usually a highly formal process.

Review the information your opponents (if you have them) are going to present. Prepare for the hearing as if it were a debate; understanding both sides of your argument will help you present your best case. Anticipate the opposition. If you know someone is going to raise an objection, do your best to defuse it before it is asked. Calmly rebut any misconceptions or misstatements.

Including Others

It can be very effective to stage a rally or a protest on the day of the hearing to bring more attention to your cause. However, if you are so noisy that nobody can hear the proceedings or so disrespectful that nobody wants to hear you, you are shortchanging yourself. Learn, teach, and model appropriate behavior. Those who lack decorum, even if they upstage the day, usually don't win in the long run.

Sometimes, however, a passionate protest rally is just what is needed to call major attention to your issue. Consider your goals. Mass action can energize supporters and demoralize opponents. But do your homework – if you are going to use public means to protest, make sure the public sees a unified organization. Nothing hurts worse than a small turnout or a counter rally staged by your own people.

Rule-making and Regulatory Agencies

Get to know the agency personnel who work on your issues. Call them to introduce yourself and explain your interest in the matter before them. Ask if you can provide information about its effect on your clients or agency. If your organization frequently is affected by rule-making or subject to regulation, it is in your best interest to develop enough of a relationship that administrative staff understand your basic concerns and can try to address them during the drafting stage of the proposed rules.

The rule-making process allows less leeway for interaction than the legislative process usually offers. It is critically important to adhere to deadlines for comments and restrictions on testimony. Because the window for comments is usually narrow and the ability to change rules once they have been drafted so slight, try to address your concerns early in the process.

If you think it will help, contact your legislators to see if they will express your concerns to administrative staff. If the issue is important enough, ask if he or she would be willing to call a meeting with the commissioner or other political appointees in the department as well as appropriate staff. Keep in mind that this approach works best when the legislator already has a good working relationship with the department in question.

HUMAN RESOURCES

CHAPTER 10

Foundation for Good Practice

People Practices

Components of Human Resources

Volunteer Management or
"Are They Worth the Trouble?"

In this chapter, we discuss the core principles involved in promoting effective and responsible management of human resources. We cover the traditional phases of employment and provide suggestions for managing the process of helping staff develop to their full potential. We focus on moving beyond a "control and compliance" mind-set for managing people toward a mission-centered model that empowers people to do their best work. The appendix includes a human resources development matrix for reviewing employee competencies within a framework that helps leaders recognize their responsibility for providing training and support to employees, for motivating staff toward increased capacity for doing well in their jobs, and for helping to determine a new set of best practices as conditions change. Finally, we provide a framework for developing an effective volunteer program.

Foundation for Good Practice

The foundation for good practice rests on the understanding that, when dealing with human resources, you have *dual responsibilities of equal importance.* You have a responsibility to ensure that people are treated fairly and given the opportunity to do their best work under the best conditions possible. At the same time, you have a responsibility to protect the organization, both legally and in the minds of stakeholders and the general public. In an ideal environment, the actions you take to protect and promote your employees will also serve to protect and promote your organization. For those unfortunate, less-than-ideal situations, it is important to have followed the law, behaved in an ethical manner, and conducted a fair and transparent process. Try to adhere to the following four practices as you attend to the human resources responsibilities of the organization.

- *Be inclusive. Within the organization,* make sure that everyone who belongs in the information loop has the opportunity to stay in the loop. Base decisions on widespread input; meetings should include as broad and representative a group as possible. Recognize that few jobs can be performed in isolation; defining a new job or changing staffing patterns should be inclusive processes that involve others in the organization in making decisions.

  Outside the organization, cast a wide net when hiring new people. Move beyond the comfortable circle of whom you know and do whatever outreach is necessary to create a talent pool. Seek expert advice when needed to avoid making well-intentioned, but wrong decisions.

- *Document your actions.* Write down your protocols for hiring. Describe the process you will use for advertising the position and who will be involved in making the decision. Develop written performance evaluation or review forms. Keep written, signed timekeeping records. Print and post workplace policies. Keep a record of steps taken when implementing disciplinary and other processes.

- *Know the law.* Ignorance of the law is no excuse for not following it. Understand what you can and cannot ask during an interview process. Put in place a clear sexual harassment policy. Become familiar with the Fair Labor Standards Act. Learn the distinction between exempt and nonexempt employees. Find out what ERISA and COBRA mean and when they apply to your organization. Contact the federal Department of Labor and the appropriate state offices for detailed information.

- *Reflect your values.* Understand that nowhere else in your organization will adherence to values reap higher rewards. Create a culture of mutual respect and open dialogue. When you care as much for the people who work for the organization as for the people the organization serves, you have set the stage for an organization without limits to what it can accomplish. Set internal standards that you would be proud to see accomplished in the outside world. Make sure that the tone and language of internal documents – even those as pedestrian as the employee handbook – fit your values.

People Practices

Personnel policies exist to ensure fair play. A core management strategy of all organizations should be to limit turnover, treat employees with respect and fairness, and inspire staff to reach new levels of thinking, decision-making, and performance. Executive directors should strive to, and be judged by, their ability to empower staff to be the best they can. They should not aim to merely "control" staff and get them to work on time.

The *principal* work of the human resource process is the continual development of processes that communicate the mission, vision, values, and hope to staff. This approach enables line staff to begin to participate in "big picture" thinking. When workers have developed a deep understanding and ownership of core values and goals, they can assume far more responsibility in the workplace. Individual staff members join a larger, ever-evolving team of people dedicated to fulfillment of the mission.

Secondary aspects of the human resource process become ensuring competency in the basic tasks listed in the job description and ensuring organizational literacy so that workers who have embraced the mission can become educated decision makers in furthering that mission. In a mission-focused (or learning) organization, staff work cooperatively to enhance the mission instead of simply performing duties.

Components of Human Resources

Program Planning and Staffing Patterns

Organizations should engage in a cooperative planning process that involves those staff who will be doing the work of the organization. To engage in such a process:

- Organizational alignment around the mission, values, and key strategies is critical. This means that the organization's mission, vision, and values should be widely understood and agreed to by the staff and other stakeholders. If this alignment does not exist, the executive director needs to do this work before attempting to institute other "people practices." (See Chapter 2, **Mission, Vision, and Values** and Chapter 3, **Program Development**.)
- All staff must be engaged in large-scale strategic planning or thinking. The executive director should ensure that the organization has designed, implemented, and disciplined itself to follow a system that incorporates planning, implementing, reflecting/evaluating, and changing – what we call "quick cycle planning." (See Chapter 5, **Strategic Planning and Thinking**.)
- The line staff should be engaged in the design of annual goals and objectives. The executive director should create the means for those closest to the work to link key program strategies with what needs to be accomplished for the next 12 months. This engages line staff in helping determine the staffing pattern needed to get the work done.

The teams of workers who deliver the services or activities should design staffing patterns. These staffing patterns and activities dictate the language that will make up job descriptions or work profiles that focus on what is needed to fulfill long-term goals and short-term activities.

Job Descriptions

Every board member, staff member, and volunteer in the organization should have a written description of what he or she is expected to do. This document should describe individual roles and responsibilities and the desired outcomes that performance can be measured against. It should also include specific tasks the job requires and the competencies needed to succeed in the position and in the organization. Competencies can include knowledge, skills, and commitments that an employee, board member, or volunteer is expected to bring to the organization.

The process for creating job descriptions is as important as the final document itself. It provides an opportunity to put into practice the principles of participation by giving the people who do the work primary responsibility for defining their jobs.

A job description in a mission-driven or learning organization should contain at least six components:

1. A restatement of the mission, values, or philosophy of service delivery, along with the stated expectation that the new employee understands and agrees to the basic approach and vision of the organization;

2. The basic duties required for this position as well as any education, experience, and competency requirements;

3. A statement of how fulfillment of these duties by the employee will bring the organization as a whole closer to its major goals and mission;

4. A statement that includes to whom the staff person reports and to which team he or she will belong;

5. The additional competencies that each "team member" will need to participate in promoting the mission and "team" nature of the workplace. For example, the job description might include statements such as:

   - All staff are expected to participate in their department's annual evaluation of its progress towards the stated goals of the team and program. Staff are expected to help shape evaluation criteria that will enable the team and the organization to evaluate their movement toward desired outcomes.

   - All staff are expected to identify and share with their team and leaders resources, such as potential donors, members, or linkages, that help the organization achieve its mission.

6. A short statement on how the organization expects the worker to hold himself or herself accountable to the expectations of the job as well as how the organization will hold him or her accountable.

Hiring Process

The hiring process, from determining the hiring committee to advertising the position, interviewing the applicants and making the decision, should reflect the culture, values, and expectations of the organization. How the organization conducts this process sets the tone for the entire relationship. Suggestions for a successful process include the following:

- Involve staff who will be working directly with the candidate in the hiring process.

- Establish the entire process ahead of time.

- Focus the first interview on whether or not the person has the skills and experience to do what the job requires.

- Focus the second interview, through hypothetical questions and scenarios, on whether the person understands and can work within the values and philosophy of service delivery that the organization supports. Keep in mind that someone with the skills and experience you need may not have the other attributes and competencies that make them a match for the organization or team. If appropriate, test for necessary skills.

- Relate your hiring needs directly to the philosophy of the overall organization and its service delivery.

Orientation and Training

Organizational culture. Every organization needs to establish an orientation process for new workers, board members, and volunteers that will ground the new member in the "culture" of the organization. This means describing the healthy and positive aspects of the culture, such as strongly held values that are translated into the expectations and day-to-day work of the staff.

Some examples:

- We are a self-help organization. Workers are trained to understand what self-help means and how not to use enabling behaviors with clients.

- We are a community-based organization. Workers will learn what community-based really means for this organization and how it translates to their day-to-day work. For example, the community is always involved in program evaluation, or the community is involved in redefining the mission and in providing feedback on planning.

Organizational literacy. Beyond the culture of the organization, the group needs to decide what will constitute organizational literacy and to develop a basic training curriculum for new staff. The executive director, along with other staff, should determine the basic knowledge about the organization and its programs that every employee should know. Schedule *ongoing* training to create literacy in the broader organizational competencies that go beyond the basic job description requirements. These competencies could include team-building, facilitation, meeting management, work with constituents, evaluation, critical thinking, and systems thinking.

Training schedule or learning plan. Each employee should have a three- to six-month training schedule or learning plan that includes when, how, and with whom he or she will be mentored, trained, and supervised. The supervisor or mentor must understand that she or he is equally responsible for the success or failure of the new worker and needs to pay close attention to the new employee during the first three months. Set aside quality time to spend with all new employees during the orientation period. On the first day, the new employee should "shadow" the mentor and be introduced to as many people as possible. Acquaint the new employee with the overall work of the organization, perhaps by arranging for attendance at staff meetings in other departments, a board meeting, volunteer training, and internal in-service training, even if it doesn't directly relate to the individual's job. If, at the end of the orientation period, the supervisor or mentor is not sure that the employee is a good match, it is better to extend the orientation period than to proceed as if it were a successful match.

Supervision, Evaluation, and Staff Development

Supervision should be structured to raise the bar on expectations – both individual and collective, so that staff members aspire to meet those expectations. Supervision should always be constructive and supportive. Group or peer supervision is best, but the whole group must be clear that when they discuss future plans, case management, progress on goals, or barriers to success, they are acting as supervisors. Every member of the group must understand that when the group sets new expectations, every individual member is responsible for meeting them.

Individual supervision should be structured so that the employee understands his or her accountability to the whole system, including his or her "contract" with his or her team members, and not just accountability to a single job description, supervisor, or boss.

Everyone needs to be trained in supervision skills; knowing when to support someone closely and when to let someone fly solo rarely comes naturally. Every individual differs in the need for guidance and motivation, and good supervisors can learn to support both the individuals and the group in moving forward.

Staff evaluations can measure quantitative as well as qualitative competencies. It is important to *document the review process*, especially if salary will be affected by the outcome. It is appropriate to evaluate specific competencies, such as whether or not – or how well – someone can write a satisfactory proposal or provide good substance abuse counseling. It is also appropriate to consider how well the person participates on the team or interacts with his or her team in working toward team goals.

The best evaluation and review processes encourage dialogue between the staff person and supervisor. The review form should be simple and straightforward and allow plenty of space for written comments. It should begin with a self-assessment that gives staff an opportunity to reflect on their performance and the kind of support and training that would allow them to rise to a new level. The written review should serve as a starting point for discussion. Discuss what kind of staff development is needed to help the employee and the organization work better. In an organization where good communication is part of the culture, the annual review will not hold any surprises for the participants.

Personnel Policies, Salaries, and Benefits

Personnel policies do not exist to punish or limit employees. Use benefits to attract the best workers, limit turnover, and make staff feel that they matter to the organization and are its most important resource. Work with the board of directors and an attorney to ensure compliance with labor laws, but provide the best, most flexible benefits possible. Use personnel policies, salary, and benefits to enhance the creation of a qualified, happy, hard-working, mission-focused staff.

In large organizations, you likely will have professional human resource staff who are well versed in employment law and practices in your field. For small organizations, while it is possible to design your own benefits package, we recommend using a broker. Ask other organizations for recommendations, and make sure that the broker you select has experience with nonprofit organizations.

Take a census of your workforce, and find out what their priorities are before designing your benefit package. Consider including low-cost benefits such as pre-tax medical, dental, and child-care plans, as well as flexible scheduling. If you include a pension benefits plan with a waiting period, consider adding a supplemental plan for employees to use during the waiting period. Use survey data for nonprofits to determine compensation ranges for your area.

Volunteer Management or "Are They Worth the Trouble?"

Many organizations could effectively involve volunteer labor if they could simply get beyond the belief that "it's not worth the trouble." A relatively small investment of time upfront can yield hundreds, if not thousands, of valuable hours of volunteer service over the life of your organization. Volunteers can do virtually any job that needs to be done. Whole organizations are run by volunteer efforts. Volunteers *are* worth the trouble. The key is to determine the organization's goals, assess the organizational needs, and take a little time to plan a viable strategy. The following framework can help you move forward.

A Framework for Effective Volunteer Programs

1. Assess your Needs. Talk to everyone – staff, board members, clients and others – about how and where volunteers can be involved in the organization. When creating a new service, consider how to involve volunteers in implementation and delivery.

2. Develop Job Descriptions and Guidelines. Create a job description for each volunteer position (as discussed in this chapter under Program Components) and include volunteers in any employee guidelines that are developed for the organization, such as technology use, confidentiality agreements, etc. Include the minimum time commitment that the position requires, e.g. one eight-hour stint; four hours per week; 15 hours each month, one day a week for at least three months, etc.

3. Develop a Record-keeping System. Recognize that volunteer hours represent a valuable in-kind contribution to your organization and make use of this information in public relations and fund development. Develop a system for keeping track of volunteer hours. Keep a folder for each volunteer that includes their application, job description, timesheets, and other relevant information.

4. Recruit. Create a simple application form that includes contact information, a statement of why the potential volunteer wants to work for the organization and which positions the volunteer is interested in, the time commitment the volunteer is prepared to make, and the qualifications the volunteer brings to the organization. Design a flier that describes volunteer opportunities and ask local organizations to post the information or distribute them to their employees and visitors. Use your community development networks to spread the word. Register with local volunteer recruitment centers and internet websites that post volunteer opportunities.

5. Interview. Make sure that every volunteer is interviewed before being "hired" in order to allow your organization and the volunteer to "check each other out" before making a commitment.

6. Provide Orientation and Training. Make sure that every volunteer receives orientation to the organization, a tour of the facility, and training for the specific position the volunteer is going to fill.

7. Ensure Job Quality and Good Volunteer Relations. Check in with volunteers and their supervisors on a periodic basis to make sure that there is enough work for the volunteer and that the volunteer's responsibilities are satisfying to the volunteer and to the staff who work with them. Take time, or make sure someone takes time, to establish and maintain a relationship with the volunteers in your organization. Consider asking one of the volunteers to take on the role of "Volunteer Coordinator."

8 Provide Supervision and Training. Make sure that volunteers receive the information and resources they need to do their jobs. Make sure that someone in the organization has responsibility for volunteer coordination and management as part of their job description. Since volunteers are often motivated by the personal and professional development they get from working in your organization, provide opportunities to participate in in-house training and self-directed learning.

9 Evaluate Volunteer Work. Feedback is as important for volunteer staff as it is for paid staff. Avoid volunteer burnout by using these check-ins to suggest changes in roles and responsibilities.

10 Provide Recognition. Celebrate your volunteers! Let them know they are appreciated. It doesn't have to be lavish; coffee and rolls, an occasional lunch ordered in, or even home-baked goods can be just as meaningful when your budget is tight. Highlight their contributions in your public relations and fund development efforts. Be ready to write letters or make calls of reference for your volunteers.

Involving volunteer workers in an organization does bring a few special concerns that must be addressed, including insurance coverage and the need to do background checks when working with vulnerable populations.

- Insurance. Volunteers are often covered by the carrier clause in an organization's insurance policy when they are involved in activities on its own property, but additional coverage may be needed if volunteers work off-site. Be especially careful about liability coverage if volunteers drive or transport clients as part of their volunteer activities. Check with your insurance company about specific policies and requirements in your area.
- Background Checks. You may be legally responsible for making sure that volunteers who work with vulnerable populations such as youth, the elderly, or disabled people, have no prior criminal history relating to abuse. Consider including in the application form a request for permission to do a criminal records check on volunteers who may work with vulnerable populations.

FINANCIAL MANAGEMENT

CHAPTER 11

This chapter focuses on one of the most critical elements of nonprofit management – managing the finances of your organization. Here we explain the importance of paying close attention to finances, describe the role and responsibilities of the executive director, and provide a primer on nonprofit financial management.

The Importance of Attention to Finances

Not every executive director will come to the job well equipped to manage finances. If you fall into the financially challenged category, don't despair. Help is available from peers, board members, service providers, and consultants. As executive director, however, you must have a sufficient knowledge base in financial management to enable you to make the best use of this outside help.

Financial management is the foundation of planning and managing every other aspect of the organization, including buildings, equipment, people, programs, fundraising, technology, printing, and insurance. Thinking strategically when managing money is essential because it is so interlinked with every other function.

A thorough understanding of your agency's finances will allow you to know if programs are cost-effective, if staffing patterns make sense, if the organization has a balanced budget, and if fund development can keep pace with the growth of the agency. Other common management questions that require a full understanding of agency finances include:

- How much revenue will our organization receive this year? Over the next three years? What portion has already been committed to the organization, and how much will we need to raise?
- What are our staffing needs, given our current and projected revenues?
- What will it cost to remain in this facility for the next five years?
- How much will it cost us to raise money this year? Over the next three years?
- What are the costs associated with operating core programs?
- What are the costs associated with developing a new initiative?
- How much will obtaining and maintaining new technology cost, including the cost of training staff in its use?
- What parts of the strategic plan are doable? Does the plan have to be revisited in light of financial analysis?
- What are the projections for health insurance costs over the next three years? Can we afford 100 percent coverage? 80 percent coverage? Can we cover family policies or only individual policies?
- Can we afford a retirement plan? If so, what type and what level of contribution can the agency support?
- Do our financial decisions reflect our organization's core values?

Be Prepared!

If you have recently taken over as executive director, be prepared for some unpleasant surprises regarding your agency's finances. In our experience, more often than not when a new executive director comes on board, she or he discovers that the financial management systems need shoring up. Even if you asked all the right questions and looked at the books and latest audit before taking the job, there is a good chance that you will find some holes that need to be patched – if not whole systems that need to be overhauled or replaced.

As soon as possible after settling into your job, we suggest that you set up a meeting with the board treasurer, your auditor or outside accountant, and your financial staff, if any. Such a meeting will help you improve your understanding of the organization's overall financial picture, including any hidden or looming financial crises, get a sense of the relative competence of the key financial players in the agency, and send a message to the entire organization that you consider financial management a high priority and will be paying close attention to it. Some of the questions for discussion at this meeting might be:

- What is your sense of the overall financial health of the organization?
- Do we have an organizational budget for the current year and projections for subsequent years?
- How is the annual budget put together?
- Do our systems produce the reports we need?
- Is there a Finance Committee and if so, who serves on it and how often does it meet? Do the members have a clear understanding of their duties?
- Is the strategic plan – assuming there is one – tightly integrated with the organization's budget?
- Are there any financial red flags out there that you should know about – revenues not collected, bills not paid, contracts not signed, lawsuits threatened or pending, accounting hardware or software issues?
- How would you rate the quality of our internal financial controls?
- Do we have the right numbers, types, and competency levels on our financial management staff?
- Has the organization ever received anything other than a clean audit? If so, when and why?

Money isn't just money. It is another lens through which we can view our organization's current reality and future potential. Money, along with mission and values, should be one of the primary screens for all organizational decisions. Executive directors and boards of directors who do not understand this – who see financial management as a necessary evil or enemy of mission and program – run the risk of jeopardizing the organization's future. Mission, money, and values are integrally connected as the core indicators for how, and at what level, programmatic actions can be taken.

Upholding fiduciary responsibility does not mean that an agency will remain forever solvent. Too many factors influence the financial health of a nonprofit organization for there to be any guarantees. Careful financial stewardship, however, will increase the likelihood of stability and will enhance the organization's credibility with all its constituents, both internal (board, staff, volunteers) and external (funders, vendors, colleagues, regulatory agencies). Confidence in the financial stability of an organization will increase the confidence of the staff to take on new challenges and make the organization a more valuable asset to the community.

Roles and Responsibilities

Financial accountability is a shared responsibility of the board of directors and the executive director. In small organizations, the board or the board and executive director may do all of the financial management. As organizations grow, their roles and responsibilities become more defined, as outlined below.

The Board of Directors

The primary role of the board is oversight. As the legally accountable entity for the entire organization, the board has overall responsibility for its financial health.

The treasurer's job is to review the organization's finances at least monthly. Some treasurers rely on monthly statements and analysis provided by the executive director, bookkeeper, or controller. Others will "open the books" once a month and do their own analysis.

Other key financial responsibilities of the board (which each individual director takes on when he or she agrees to be a member of the board), include:

- *Approving the annual budget* (and helping to design it in small organizations). The annual budget should use realistic (conservative) projections for revenue to help ensure that the organization does not end up with an unexpected deficit.

  The budget should include expense line items that set the parameters within which the executive director can operate. We recommend a board-established policy that allows for a modest variance (generally 5 percent to 10 percent) for each line item, so that the executive director does not have to alert the board to minor variances, as long as the bottom line does not change. *If the organization is being managed within these parameters, the board's financial oversight responsibility should be limited to monitoring.* Unless there are serious problems or the executive director or treasurer requests help, micromanagement of finances by the board is usually counterproductive and not in best interests of the organization.

The board's fiduciary responsibility and its role in approving or setting the annual budget carries with it the responsibility to provide fair and equitable salaries, benefits, working conditions, facilities, and resources. Typically, the board sets the parameters for these matters and hires an executive director to manage and implement them.

- *Ensuring that the agency has adequate funds* to operate on an annual basis.
- *Ensuring that all financial reports, taxes, and other government requirements are met by the agency.*
- *Establishing policies and procedures designed to assure overall accountability* for programs and finances and adequate systems to implement them.
- *Choosing and contracting with a CPA to conduct an audit on an annual basis.* While we believe it is good practice to conduct an annual audit, check with your state attorney general's office to find out if you are required to have one. In Massachusetts, for example, you are required to have an annual audit if your annual budget is over $250,000 and a financial review if your annual budget is between $100,000 and $250,000. The board's decision regarding the auditor should be duly recorded each year in the minutes. It is generally a good idea to put your audit out to bid every few years to make sure you are getting the best price and also to have the benefit of a different perspective on your financial operations.
- *Ensuring ongoing fiscal monitoring.* This role is extremely important because of the liability associated with a failure to exercise appropriate financial oversight. As stated above, the treasurer should carefully review the books monthly and report to the board at its regular meetings. A regular treasurer's report to the board of directors is the foundation of the checks and balances system that guarantees full financial disclosure and accountability. In the event of a financial crisis or serious irregularity, the treasurer should inform the president and, if necessary, request a special board meeting.

  If a board of directors does nothing else, it should convene to hear the treasurer's report and approve it if it makes sense. (The legal test is that it must make sense to the mind of any ordinary, prudent person.) If the report does not make sense in some way, it should be questioned. Any corrective actions should be put in the notes and minutes. The treasurer and/or finance committee should monitor the executive director's management of corrective action.

  While the board holds ultimate fiduciary responsibility, it is the responsibility of both the board and the executive director to ensure the organization's viability and fiscal accountability.

The Executive Director

The primary responsibility of the executive director is to understand the organization's finances, interpret them for other stakeholders, and, together with the board, see that the agency remains financial accountable to its community.

Typically, the board delegates responsibility for managing the functions that fulfill its role in meeting legal requirements to the executive director, who handles the actual contracting with auditors and the filing of legal forms, such as annual reports, tax returns, etc. The executive director, in turn, often delegates these functions to staff and consultants, depending on the size of the organization. The executive director must have a basic understanding of bookkeeping and nonprofit financial management. She or he should be able to read a budget, monthly financial statements, and audit reports and be able to understand, and sometimes develop, internal financial management systems and controls. In addition, the executive director should know how to project the agency's financial needs against its fundraising capacity.

In smaller organizations, where the budget does not support a separate financial management staff, the executive director typically takes on all the work of the financial manager as well.

Be honest with yourself. If you are not skilled at financial projections, monitoring, building meaningful budgets (operating, capital, and fundraising), and creating sound financial management systems, *and* you don't have other staff who can do these things, get support from the board or community and meet monthly with people who can help you with your overall financial management responsibilities. *No executive director will have every skill required for the range of nonprofit management functions.* If your strengths lie elsewhere, find partners to help with financial management. Take a course from a nonprofit training center or local college.

In very small nonprofits the executive director or a board member is often also the bookkeeper. Note, however, that this is not a good situation – primarily for ethical reasons. If you find yourself in this situation, ask a local auditor (even if your organization is too small to require an audit) to give some pro bono time to analyze your financial management system and recommend appropriate checks and balances.

The Financial Manager

Some organizations have a large enough or flexible enough budget to employ a financial manager or controller. A financial manager can handle many tasks that would otherwise fall to the executive director, treasurer, and finance committee. A financial manager maintains the general ledger and can prepare budget drafts, develop financial management and monitoring systems, and assist with the financial details of human resource issues, such as retirement funds, health benefits, Section 125 plans, and cost of living projections and salary increases. The financial manager can shop for better buys, research accounting software, monitor monthly expenses by line item, generate financial reports at the level required by the board of directors, monitor cash flow, assist with the budgets of funding contracts, and prepare reports to funders as required. In some cases, the financial manager will also do all the basic bookkeeping.

The Bookkeeper

Many organizations have dedicated and highly skilled bookkeepers who do many of the tasks described above. The basic responsibilities of the bookkeeper, however, are to record income and expenses according to generally accepted accounting methods, create and maintain simple financial systems that enable the accurate recording of income and expenses on a monthly basis, prepare billings to funders and other customers, produce clear reports to the executive director and board of directors, typically on a monthly basis, and produce needed documents for the auditor on an annual basis.

Staffing Considerations

The way financial management tasks are handled in an organization often depends on the size of the budget and, especially in smaller organizations, on the competencies of the staff. An executive director who is a generalist and doing many other things should dedicate on average one to one-and-a-half days every two weeks to all the tasks related to financial management. Keep in mind, however, this will only cover the basics.

With the widespread use of computers, the time needed by nonprofits for bookkeeping has been slashed dramatically. An experienced bookkeeper working with an organization that has sound financial systems, a modest number of government contracts, and a budget under $1 million should be able to fulfill basic bookkeeping responsibilities in 8 to 10 hours per week. However, even a $1 million organization might need considerably more bookkeeping time, up to a full-time position, if it has multiple funding streams and/or government contracts that include strict budget and reporting requirements.

A growing, mid-sized nonprofit should consider hiring a full-time financial manager or experienced bookkeeper who can handle all the details. Such an action can free the executive director to provide general management of this function and to position the organization for a more mature pattern of growth through sound financial practice. By the time an organization has reached the $2+ million level, a full-time accounting position is usually justified, especially if the organization's finances are fairly complex (multiple state and federal contracts, ongoing fundraising campaigns that involve pledging, multiple sites or management of multiple facilities). Organizations of this size often need a half-time bookkeeping position as well. Larger nonprofits (over $5 million) typically require a finance department that includes a controller, staff accountant, and bookkeeper.

Beware of the tendency to overstaff. Agencies with flexibility in their budgets, an executive director with little or no financial experience, and a board that is not as engaged in its fiduciary responsibilities as it should be often find themselves hiring paid staff instead of reengaging the board or providing training for the executive director. Keep in mind that an organization is not well served if its leadership is allowed to abdicate its responsibility for financial management. A good auditor or financial consultant can review your agency's financial needs and give you and the board a sense of what present and future staffing patterns should be.

The Basics

Cash or Accrual Accounting?

Your organization will need to choose between cash and accrual accounting. Cash basis accounting and reporting reflects only transactions involving cash. Accrual basis accounting reflects cash transactions, but also includes revenues earned but not yet received and expenses incurred but not yet paid. Under the cash method, an organization's fund balance can be significantly overstated or understated, since it does not account for amounts owed to or from others. We recommend the accrual method for most organizations because it provides a more accurate view of the organization's financial position for a specific accounting period.

Developing an Operating Budget – More Left Brain than You Think!

Developing budgets is actually fairly easy. Most organizations will build off actual costs from the previous year. Start by taking all of the line items from the previous year and adding any new costs. Salary and benefit changes are usually the most complex to project. Keep in mind that there will likely be changes during the year – unexpected turnover, new funding that allows a long-dreamed-for position to be filled, or budget cuts – but projections must be as realistic as possible. All other line items can be built by factoring in estimated inflation and any substantial changes in programming, facilities, staffing, or equipment. If, for instance, you have purchased 10 new computers, include the effect on the office supplies line item, possibly on utilities (more electricity consumed) and on staff training.

Follow the same procedure with the income side of the budget sheet. *Your fund development plan for the next budget year should be in place before you develop the operating budget.* Link income and expense projections. The capacity to raise funds comes first, however. (See Chapter 7, **Fund Development**.) The organization's operating budget *should never exceed* the fund development goal.

The safest method for developing an operating budget is to use conservative figures for fundraising totals and slightly inflated figures for expense totals. *Do not fall into the trap* of picking a wishful revenue figure and assuming the agency will somehow raise it all.

If managers or team leaders are involved in developing department or team budgets, give them the previous year's expenses to build from and include some financial parameters; otherwise, they may include unrealistic costs. Encouraging them to create the income side of the balance sheet as well will help them understand that the agency cannot spend money it does not raise.

Who should develop the operating budget? While the board should set the budget parameters, having staff and board representatives involved in developing the budget will increase buy-in at different levels. When the staff and board understand the true cost of doing business, they tend to be more understanding of budget constraints (such as smaller raises) and more inclined to assist in fund development. If your organization is so small that its managers cannot take time to participate in the budget process, try to include at least one other person in addition to the executive director and the finance committee in developing the budget.

Sample Operating Budget	FY 2001	FY 2002	FY 2003
Line Items	Amounts		
Revenues			
State contracts	625,000	656,250	689,063
Membership dues	25,000	27,500	30,250
Contributions	80,000	88,000	98,000
Service fees	170,000	178,500	187,425
Foundation grants	300,000	325,000	350,000
Other	0	0	0
Total Revenues	**1,200,000**	**1,275,250**	**1,354,738**
Expenses			
Salaries & wages	760,000	798,000	837,900
Employee benefits	152,000	159,600	167,580
Consultants	110,000	110,000	110,000
Rent	60,000	75,000	75,000
Utilities	3,600	3,780	3,969
Equipment maintenance	4,200	4,410	4,631
Insurance	20,000	21,000	22,050
Travel	7,000	7,350	7,718
Telephone	4,000	4,200	4,410
Postage	7,000	7,350	7,718
Office supplies	4,200	4,410	4,631
Printing	12,500	13,125	13,781
Staff recruitment	6,000	6,300	6,615
Professional fees	14,000	14,700	15,435
Training and development	6,000	6,300	6,615
Miscellaneous	6,000	6,000	6,000
Other	0	0	0
Total Expenses	**1,176,500**	**1,241,525**	**1,294,051**
Surplus/Deficit (-)	**23,500**	**33,725**	**60,686**

Indirect Cost Calculations

The basic formula looks like this:

A. **Total agency indirect costs / Total agency direct program costs = Indirect cost rate**

B. **Indirect cost rate x Individual program direct costs = Program indirect costs**

C. **Program direct costs + Program indirect costs = Total program expenses**

Calculating and Covering Indirect Costs

Indirect costs are costs that benefit all programs but cannot be easily identified as relating to a specific program. Indirect costs might include the salaries and benefits of administrative staff such as the executive director, accountant, and receptionist, as well as payroll service costs, insurance, rent, and other costs related to the administrative function of the organization.

Indirect costs are generally pooled into one cost center and then assigned proportionately to specific programs. Start by adding up all of your indirect costs. Then, add up all of your direct program costs. Direct program costs include program salaries, fringe benefits, and consulting fees, as well as printing, travel, or other identifiable, line-item costs attributable to specific programs. Next, divide the total of all indirect costs by the total of all program direct costs. This will give you an indirect cost rate. You can then multiply this percentage by the total direct cost for each individual program to get the amount of indirect costs to be added to direct costs in order to get a total program expense budget.

A grant or contract that covers only direct costs such as staff, consultants, and travel but none, or only part, of the indirect costs borne by the program can be a loss leader. Sometimes, to meet the mission of the organization, it is important to accept a loss leader type of grant. Many agencies do. There must, however, be a plan for covering in some other way the indirect costs related to the grant and the program it is supporting. Make sure you include these costs in your fund development budget. If your organization receives direct federal funding, you should apply for a negotiated rate in order to receive reimbursement for indirect costs. Contact the federal awarding agency for information on establishing indirect cost rates.

Capital Budgets

A capital budget consists of items that an organization has purchased or plans to purchase that will have a useful life of longer than one year and a cost greater than a threshold established by the organization. Items in the capital budget – typically buildings and costly equipment – are listed as assets in the organization's financial records and are depreciated, or capitalized, over a predetermined "useful" life. This means that a portion of the cost is listed as an expense in each year of its useful life. For example, suppose you buy a piece of equipment with a useful life of four years. Every year, for four years, you would record one-fourth of the original cost as a depreciation expense. At the end of four years, the piece of equipment would be fully depreciated and would not be considered an asset on your books, even though you might still be using it. The useful life of most equipment has been predetermined by tax law or accounting convention, so if you are in doubt, check with an accountant or the IRS.

Most organizations set a threshold for items that will appear on the capital budget so that they don't have to go through the trouble of depreciating the cost of numerous small items. Common thresholds are $3,000 to $5,000 for a piece of equipment. Items that fall below the threshold are listed as one-time expenses in the annual operating budget.

Capital budget items usually will need to be replaced when they have worn out or become obsolete, so be sure to budget for the replacement cost. The use of a capital budget and depreciation schedule can serve to remind you to set aside an amount in reserve – perhaps equal to the amount being depreciated – so that you will have the resources available when it is time to replace old equipment.

Budgets in the Board Room

Although the treasurer should review the more detailed working budgets that the executive director, bookkeeper, and financial manager work with on a day-to-day basis, the full board should review only the aggregate totals for various line items on a monthly or regular basis. For example, if $500 per month is set aside for printing, the treasurer may want to know how those funds were spent in the last quarter. The full board, however, needs to know only that the treasurer has reviewed the books for the month (or quarter) and that no line items are substantially off target.

The Art of Cash Flow

Cash flow has become an increasingly large problem for nonprofit organizations that receive a significant percentage of their income from cost-reimbursement contracts. Payments from public agencies may lag behind expenses by three to six months.

If your agency is eligible for a federal letter of credit or up-front payments from state agencies (called "ready pay" in Massachusetts), you can eliminate a great deal of your cash flow problems. If not, you may need to seek a line of credit from a bank, which of course carries a cost in the form of interest. For this reason, *it is very important to examine the financial implications of cost-reimbursement contracts before accepting them.*

A cash flow budget is a useful tool for organizations without large cash reserves because it enables you to predict your monthly cash needs over the course of the year and plan ahead for the dry periods.

It is fairly simple to put together a cash flow budget. Start with the unrestricted cash available at the beginning of the fiscal year. Next, list all the income anticipated each month against all anticipated payments. Typically, contract-dependent agencies will have dry periods with no cash coming in. During these months, it is necessary to dip into reserves (borrow from the reserve account to pay current operating expenses) or borrow against a line of credit.

If possible, do not carry an ongoing line of credit. Always pay it off as soon as possible. Nonprofit organizations too often find themselves in situations (much like individuals with credit cards) in which they cannot get ahead enough to pay off the line of credit, and then begin having to budget for ever-increasing interest costs.

Cash Flow Forecast - 12 Months														
Month	**Cash on Hand**	**1**	**2**	**3**	**4**	**5**	**6**	**7**	**8**	**9**	**10**	**11**	**12**	**Totals**
Revenues														
State contracts		0	25,000	75,000	60,000	100,000	40,000	30,000	60,000	80,000	55,000	40,000	60,000	625,000
Membership dues		1,000	0	0	0	0	2,500	10,000	6,000	3,000	1,500	1,000	0	25,000
Contributions		2,000	2,000	5,000	6,000	10,000	30,000	10,000	5,000	4,000	3,000	2,000	1,000	80,000
Service fees		10,000	12,000	18,000	18,000	18,000	8,000	8,000	15,000	18,000	15,000	18,000	12,000	170,000
Foundation grants		15,000	0	25,000	40,000	75,000	15,000	10,000	50,000	10,000	35,000	15,000	10,000	300,000
Other		0	0	0	0	0	0	0	0	0	0	0	0	0
Total Revenues	**25,000**	**28,000**	**39,000**	**123,000**	**124,000**	**203,000**	**95,500**	**68,000**	**136,000**	**115,000**	**109,500**	**76,000**	**83,000**	**1,200,000**
Expenses														
Salaries & wages		55,000	55,000	65,000	75,000	75,000	75,000	75,000	65,000	60,000	60,000	50,000	50,000	760,000
Employee benefits		11,000	11,000	13,000	15,000	15,000	15,000	15,000	13,000	12,000	12,000	10,000	10,000	152,000
Consultants		5,000	5,000	5,000	10,000	10,000	5,000	5,000	15,000	10,000	20,000	15,000	5,000	110,000
Rent		5,000	5,000	5,000	5,000	5,000	5,000	5,000	5,000	5,000	5,000	5,000	5,000	60,000
Utilities		300	300	300	300	300	300	300	300	300	300	300	300	3,600
Equipment maintenance		350	350	350	350	350	350	350	350	350	350	350	350	4,200
Insurance		5,000	0	0	5,000	0	0	5,000	0	0	5,000	0	0	20,000
Travel		250	250	500	1,500	1,500	250	500	500	500	500	500	250	7,000
Telephone		250	250	500	500	500	250	250	250	250	250	250	500	4,000
Postage		150	150	1,200	750	250	1,500	150	300	1,500	750	150	150	7,000
Office supplies		350	350	350	350	350	350	350	350	350	350	350	350	4,200
Printing		0	0	6,000	2,000	0	0	0	0	3,000	1,000	500	0	12,500
Staff recruitment		0	0	1,500	0	0	1,500	0	0	1,500	0	1,500	0	6,000
Professional fees		0	2,000	8,000	1,000	0	0	0	1,000	1,000	1,000	0	0	14,000
Training and development		0	0	0	1,200	1,200	0	1,200	0	0	1,200	1,200	0	6,000
Miscellaneous		500	500	500	500	500	500	500	500	500	500	500	500	6,000
Other		0	0	0	0	0	0	0	0	0	0	0	0	0
Total expenses	**0**	**83,150**	**80,150**	**107,200**	**118,450**	**109,950**	**105,000**	**108,600**	**101,550**	**96,250**	**108,200**	**85,600**	**72,400**	**1,176,500**
Cashflow Surplus/Deficit (-)	**25,000**	**-55,150**	**-41,150**	**15,800**	**5,550**	**93,050**	**-9,500**	**-40,600**	**34,450**	**18,750**	**1,300**	**-9,600**	**10,600**	**23,500**
Opening Cash Balance	**0**	**25,000**	**-30,150**	**-71,300**	**-55,500**	**-49,950**	**43,100**	**33,600**	**-7,000**	**27,450**	**46,200**	**47,500**	**37,900**	
Closing Cash Balance	**25,000**	**-30,150**	**-71,300**	**-55,500**	**-49,950**	**43,100**	**33,600**	**-7,000**	**27,450**	**46,200**	**47,500**	**37,900**	**48,500**	

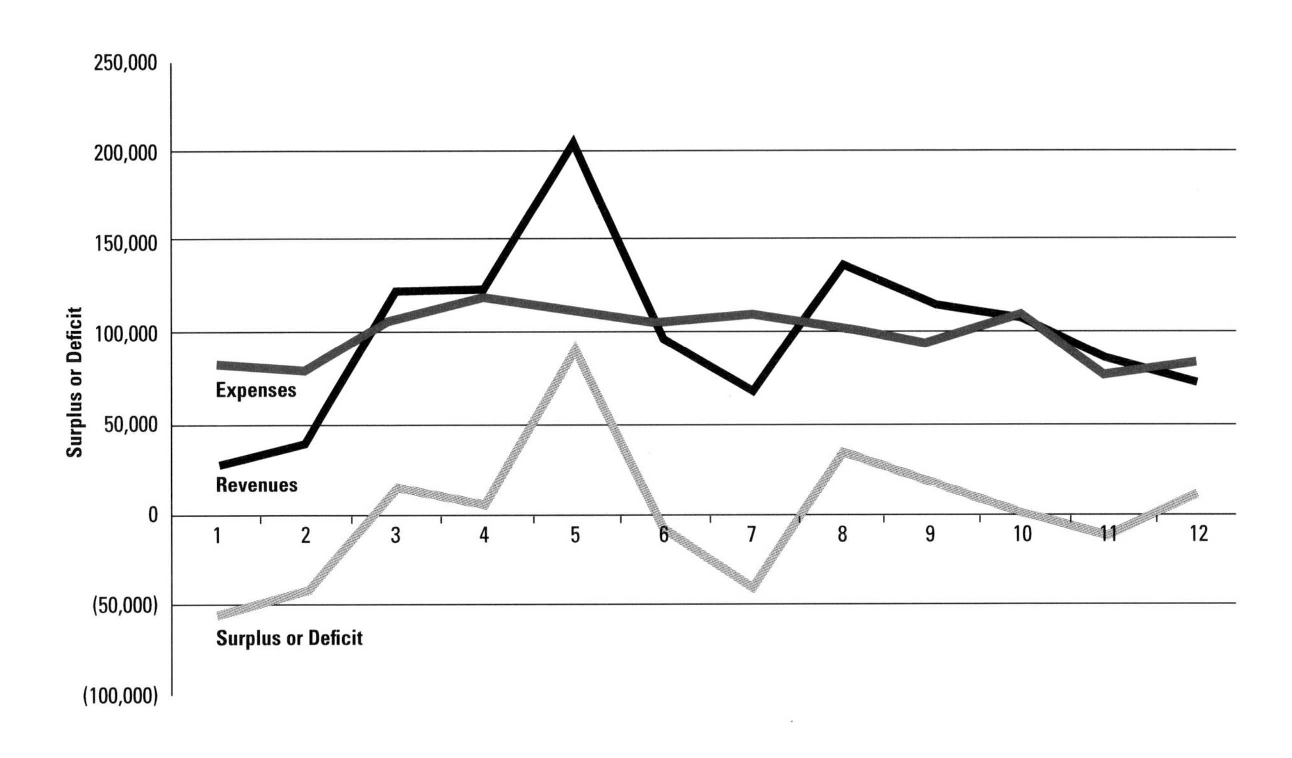

The Auditor as Friend

As we stated at the beginning of this chapter, one of the first meetings a new executive director should have is with the auditor. Inexperienced executives moan and groan about audits, but experienced ones use the audit to their advantage. *A good auditor is one of your organization's best friends.*

While the IRS does not require an annual certified audit, many states do. Most funders will ask for copies of the audit. It should also be part of the packet you give to prospective board members.

How to find an auditor. An auditor is a certified public accountant. Make sure yours has experience with nonprofit organizations since many accounting rules apply only to nonprofits. Experience in your field of work is even better. Check with your state's association of nonprofits, or ask other executive directors for recommendations.

What to ask your auditor. The auditor's job is to express an opinion on the organization's statement of financial position in accordance with generally accepted auditing standards and any applicable government standards. Ask how your organization can design its financial systems in order to meet those standards and regulations. Usually, money spent to put appropriate systems in place will save money down the line.

During the audit, keep an eye out for the coming year. Ask the auditor what the agency is doing right and wrong. Can you improve your system of internal controls? What work can be done internally to better prepare your organization for the audit and to reduce its cost?

How to prepare for the audit. Before scheduling the audit, your auditor will send you a list of items to assemble. These will include copies of financial statements, trial balances, supporting schedules, board minutes, leases, loan agreements, depreciation schedules, accounting policies and procedures, grant awards, and contracts. Auditors will also need access to all documents supporting the organization's financial transactions. Collect all reports to government agencies and have all financial files easily accessible. Make sure time sheets and other payroll records are complete and in order. Prepare a list of assets, including equipment, property, inventory, and money that is owed to you, and a list of liabilities. Pull together all bank statements, checkbooks, and canceled checks. Make a list of all donations and donors.

What to expect from your auditor. If an organization has done what it is contracted to do, maintained good financial systems with appropriate checks and balances, kept orderly books, submitted its reports to the attorney general, the IRS, funders, and any regulatory bodies in a timely manner, maintained ethical standards in fundraising, and expended funds as approved by the board for the defined mission and program, then it should have no problems with the audit. During the audit, your auditor will:

- review internal controls for the approval of expenditures and safeguarding of assets;
- test entries in the general ledger and verify their authenticity by inspection of vouchers, bills, checks, invoices, and other documents;
- test fulfillment of service contracts by reviewing time sheets to ensure staff were assigned to programs as required by the project, invoices, travel requests, and financial and narrative reports;
- verify asset and liability balances by sending confirmation letters to bank and investment firms; and
- review proper compliance with tax law, annual reporting, and maintenance of tax-exempt status.

If federally funded program expenses exceed $300,000, the auditor may also be required to conduct a compliance audit (an "A-133" audit) of federally funded programs administered by your organization.

The Art of Financial Management

Accounting is not as black and white as it might appear on the surface. There is always room for interpretation – within, however, highly prescriptive accounting parameters. What is sometimes called creative accounting is actually strategic use of financial management – as long as it stays within the boundaries of good practice. When in doubt, interpret narrowly. Recognize your auditor as an important resource in developing the strategic dimension of your financial skills. The rules of accounting change often, and your auditor can help you work through the changing world.

TECHNOLOGY PLANNING

CHAPTER 12

As more and more people become regular users of information technology and are aware of all that it has to offer, nonprofit organizations are feeling the need to become more technologically literate and to create an Internet presence for their organizations. We applaud that effort; technology will continue to grow in importance as a communication tool as well as an information management tool.

Today, anyone going on the Web to look for information about technology and nonprofit organizations will find hundreds of websites – so many that it can be a chore just sifting through them. We won't attempt to duplicate them here. Instead, our goal in this chapter is to help you think about the issues you should consider and guide you in developing a plan for addressing them.

Computer software and hardware change so quickly that any reference to specific products would become outdated quickly. Rather, we will help you understand how to determine your technology needs and make informed decisions about allocating resources.

Technology Planning

Every organization needs to think strategically about the role of technology in its work. Technology planning is the process of bringing together staff, board members, clients, and other stakeholders to determine the role of technology in fulfilling the mission of your organization. Whether your organization has fully embraced technology or is taking its first steps toward a more technology-based future, it is important to decide *collectively* where you are going, what your needs will be, and how you will get there.

The *process* of developing a technology plan has three main goals:

- to create guidelines for technology use in the future;
- to open a dialogue on incorporating technology into the practices and programming of the organization; and
- to engage a broad spectrum of stakeholders who will understand and support technology integration throughout the organization.

A thoughtful and inclusive planning process will yield a versatile document that allows the organization to navigate smoothly in the ever-changing environment of information technology. More specifically, a well-developed technology plan[1] can help you:

- guide your budget process and annual expenditures, since you will know ahead of time what equipment and training is needed;
- lower costs through an in-house analysis that identifies gaps;
- lower costs through planning that focuses on your organization's goals and not just on the available technology;
- reduce disruptions from staff turnover, which can be a problem when few people in the organization have knowledge about technology;
- establish a training agenda; without a clear plan, training is often haphazard or nonexistent;
- decide whether to accept or reject in-kind donations;
- know better where and when to collaborate;
- make strategic decisions about new products and services as they become available; and
- make fundraising for technology needs a clear and coherent process.

Steps in Planning

A technology plan should be an organic document. It is not something to be developed and put on a shelf, never to be referred to again. Technology planning is much like strategic planning; it works best

[1] Thanks to Chris Sullivan of the Minnesota Council of Nonprofits (*www.mncn.org*) for permission to adapt several slides and key points from his presentation "Strategic Technology Planning."

when it is based on strategic *thinking*. (See Chapter 5, **Strategic Planning and Thinking**.) If technology planning hasn't been integrated into your strategic planning process, it may be necessary to jump-start the organization with a plan that focuses more directly on technology.

1 Plan to plan. Identify the stakeholders among board, staff, clients, and others who should and/or would like to participate in the planning process, including line staff, technology enthusiasts and development staff. Set a time line for developing the plan. Decide on ground rules; for example, technology should support the mission and not be seen as an end in itself. Assess whether you have someone on staff with the expertise needed to develop the technical aspects of the plan. Consider bringing in a consultant to facilitate the process and to help make sure that you cover everything necessary to create a workable plan. If you decide to bring in a consultant, look for one with experience in nonprofit organizational development as well as expertise in technology.

2 Assess current reality. Assess the current role of technology in your organization; have your needs already been identified? Consider what is driving the effort to develop a technology plan; is there organizational buy-in to the need to spend time on the effort? Consider the budget realities; what level of funding is available in the current budget, and what new sources for funding have been identified? Assess the staff's capabilities and willingness to learn; some organizations ask for a technical skills assessment of new employees or volunteers to identify skills and training needs. Make sure there will be people on staff who can assume responsibility for technology development; volunteers are great, but you should never depend on just one person – especially if that person is a volunteer. Assess the needs of the client base; can an investment in technology improve services to clients or help clients develop their own skills?

3 Consider the economic, social, and demographic environments that influence the organization and how they will affect the need for, and use of, information technology. Work with stakeholders to determine how broad the parameters of the plan should be; a technology plan can range from a simple review of office equipment needs to a comprehensive community-development-via-the-Web strategy. Ask how far and how fast the organization wants to push itself and its client base.

4 Define the role of information technology in your organization. Survey the staff and board to learn what they have identified as technology *needs* that would help them do their jobs effectively, *wants* that would help them do more than their current jobs allow, and *goals* that would make the organization ready for the future. Ask others outside the organization to suggest possibilities that might not have been considered in-house. Develop the long-term strategic and short-term functional goals for technology within the organization. Develop general policies and procedures.

5 Design a system for monitoring the plan and evaluating progress on stated goals and activities. Require people to check in with the plan before making purchases. Review the plan when technology questions arise. Avoid independent decision making; this is one area where we advocate centralized authority, as long as it follows the decisions reached in the group planning process.

6 Make the plan operational. Prioritize the goals (short- and long-term) and include the key steps needed to accomplish them. Attach time lines to activities; the best intentions will fall by the wayside in light of more immediate day-to-day issues. Attach people to responsibilities so that everyone is clear about who will do what and who will make or sign off on key decisions. Create a budget that includes the costs of hardware, software, and training. Build it into your annual budget.

7 Implement. Make sure everyone knows that the plan exists to be acted upon. Demonstrate your commitment to it. Check in with the people who have taken on responsibility for implementation. If areas of the plan need more detail in order to be implemented by the target dates assigned, make sure that the people attached

to the responsibilities listed are meeting in small groups or task forces to design and implement a manageable agenda.

Policies and Procedures

A good starting point for developing policies and strategies as part of your technology plan is to review all existing policies and procedures that relate to technology usage. Have isolated policies been implemented to deal with specific situations? The main point, whether covered in a technology plan or employee handbook, is to address issues fairly and reasonably and to make sure policies are widely distributed and understood throughout the organization. In general, we recommend a light touch when regulating the use of computer technology applications or the Internet in order to encourage employees to use and become comfortable with them. Keep in mind that along with the policies themselves, it is important to *work with the staff* to make policies as useful as possible and to let people understand the reasons for the policies.

Computer-use Policies

Computer-use policies should encourage enough use to promote computer fluency but ensure respectful conduct in the workplace. In addition, computer-use policies should be compatible with personal-use policies. For example, if you allow reasonable use of the telephone for personal business, you may wish to do the same with e-mail or surfing the Web. Other computer-use issues to address include respecting the privacy of client records, defining protocols for storing and saving files (especially important when employees must access common files), sharing equipment, handling viruses (frequency of updating virus protection, when not to open e-mail attachments, etc.), security, recycling of old equipment, and inappropriate Internet content.

Disaster Recovery Procedures

Backup.
Backup.
Backup.
Make sure you have procedures in place for backing up all of your data regularly. And then make sure that your backup protocols are tested periodically to ensure that they are working. You should keep an extra copy of your backup files at another location away from your main place of business. In addition, keep a paper copy of key documents and records.

Training Policies

To ensure that all members of your organization are truly effective users of information technology:

- Make computer training a priority.
- Establish monetary goals for spending on training and let the staff know that it is one budget area that you *want* "zeroed out" by the end of the year.
- Simplify the process for staff who want to get training.
- Talk to staff and find out what kind of training works best for them.
- Bring trainers on-site to work with staff members who have specific needs and little free time.
- Ask all new staff and volunteers to do a skills assessment and then design a training schedule for them to fill in the gaps in their knowledge and help them gain new skills.
- Assign a computer mentor to staff with weak technology skills.
- Ask staff to identify the training that they received over the past year and to set goals for training during the coming year as part of the annual review.
- Institute a policy requiring that more than one person develop each computer skill needed by the organization in order to minimize the effect of staff turnover on technological literacy.

Equipment Needs

No matter how technology-oriented you want your organization to become, keep in mind that it is people who make it all work. New machines can change the way people do their jobs, but the change will be for the better only if the needs and habits of the people who use them are taken into account. We believe that technology should be used whenever possible to expand an organization's capacity to uphold its mission by operating in new and innovative ways. It should be used, however, in ways that simplify and streamline the work process and that do not add unnecessary complications to the already overloaded workday of nonprofit staff.

The first step in determining your equipment needs is to *conduct an assessment* of what you already have. Tedious though it may be to do, it *is* necessary. Besides giving you a solid foundation for future decision making, it will be useful to have for insurance purposes. Itemize every piece of equipment, and collect every packing slip and order form as it is acquired. Make your assessment as detailed and thorough as possible. And then keep it current.

Hardware

Computer hardware is evolving so fast that new equipment is likely to be obsolete in three years. For that reason, we recommend buying as close to the cutting edge as possible when it suits your needs to do so. While some innovations are much more costly in the first year of availability, keep in mind that you will never get ahead of the curve when buying hardware. On the other hand, you may never have an organizational need for a new type or updated version of equipment, and it does not make sense to have the best of something you do not need. So, the best strategy is to stick to your plan; use technology for meeting your mission and buy only what you need.

The basics of hardware include the following:

- *The processor or central processing unit* (CPU) determines how fast the computer runs and accomplishes tasks. It is measured in megahertz (MHz) or gigahertz (GHz), and the numbers are going up all the time.
- *Memory* affects how fast your computer *programs* work and how many of them can work at once. Memory is measured in megabytes. When purchasing hardware, make sure the memory can be expanded or upgraded to at least four times its initial size.
- The *hard drive* is where program files, such as your word processing files, are stored. The hard drive is measured in gigabytes.
- The *motherboard* is the part of the computer that connects all of the various pieces of the computer. For example, the CPU sits on the motherboard.
- *Expansion slots* allow you to add optional equipment, such as a modem or video card, to your computer. Most computers have four or five expansion slots built in.
- A *video card* is used for creating graphics and brochures and for playing games. It translates information between your screen and your motherboard and can create 3D images.
- A *sound card* allows you to hear what is available on certain sites or video games. If you don't have speakers to plug into the sound card, you will need to use headphones (most computers come with a plug for headphones) or get external speakers in order to hear sound.
- *CD-ROM* drive or *DVD-ROM* drive enables you to use compact disks with your computer. DVD technology is becoming increasingly available and will read CD-ROM. DVD disks hold enough information to allow you to watch a movie through your computer.
- *CD writers* allow you to store (write) information to a compact disk, which can hold almost 500 times as much information as a floppy disk and can easily transfer information to other computers. CD *readers* copy information permanently and cannot be overridden or edited. CD *readers/writers* act more like floppy disks and can be edited, erased, copied over, etc. Older computers have a hard time reading CD-RWs.
- *Networks* allow people at different computers to share printers, files, databases, and access to the Internet. Simple networks connect small groups of computers through a hub and allow them to transfer files from one to another. Simple networks require each computer to have a *network card* installed in an expansion slot and connected to the motherboard, and for each computer to be attached with a cable to a common hub. More complex hubs need a *server* (a big hub) that stores common files, holds programs, and allows one central backup each

night (or more often). Each computer is attached to the hub. When the network grows too large for a single hub, another hub is needed, and the hubs are attached to each other.

- *Hubs* typically connect 2 to 24 computers together and can share a connection to the Internet. More expensive hubs are *switched* to allow them to work "smarter" than normal hubs. They work faster than normal hubs by routing network information better.
- *Modems* are used to connect your computer to the Internet. In a small network, each computer can have its own modem and telephone line to connect to the Internet through an *Internet service provider* (ISP). (If all computers share one telephone line, only one person can be using the Internet at a time unless they include a device that allows them to share an Internet connection.) The next step in service is a DSL line, which provides continuous Internet access (without having to dial up) through a telephone line and a DSL-capable modem. Cable modems also provide continuous Internet access through a coaxial or television cable. T-1 lines provide a direct connection to the Internet, as do T-3 lines (which can cost thousands of dollars to lease). Once you make a decision to use an Internet connection that is on all of the time, security becomes a bigger issue, and steps must be taken to install good security software and firewalls to restrict access.
- *Bandwidth* is a way of describing how fast an Internet connection will be. A typical modem speed is 56K. Cable modems and DSL will be up to 10 times faster than that. A T-1 line can be even faster.
- *Scanners, printers, and fax machines* work best as separate pieces of equipment instead of the all-in-one desktop versions that are also available.

Software

The activities of your organization will determine which software you need. Think about the needs of your staff and do not let software companies, through their upgrades, always make the decision for you. If everyone is satisfied with the current version, consider riding with it until the upgrade is so compelling that you can't help but change. The basic issues to keep in mind when purchasing software are compatibility among computer users, ease of use, and ability to perform the functions you have need for in your organization. Give consideration to compatibility with board members, volunteers, clients and collaborators; sharing documents is easier if you all use the same software. Common software needs include:

- word processing;
- spreadsheets or accounting capability;
- databases;
- e-mail and Internet browsers;
- desktop publishing; and
- text-recognition software for use with a scanner.

Smaller organizations should think twice about purchasing software that has been custom designed for them. While there are times when it makes sense to do so, keep in mind that such a purchase will keep you tied to the vendor who designed it for as long as you use the software. Consider the long-term implications when making the decision.

Internet Presence

The first step is to determine whether the organization has a purpose for creating an Internet presence. Do you have information that would be useful to anyone – customers, clients, other organizations, etc. – if you put it on the Web? Consider staff time constraints and technological ability in making the decision to create a website. Maintaining a website can be very labor-intensive.

A website can function as little more than an online brochure, or it can provide continuously updated information about organizational activities and opportunities for interaction with clients, supporters, other organizations, and community groups. Whatever your organization decides, make sure that the site is clear and uncluttered and that information is up-to-date, concise, and easy to access. Keep your audience in mind and solicit feedback at every stage of development.

Developing and maintaining a website can be done:

- in-house with staff that has received the necessary training;
- with a paid consultant who has experience in website development and whose work you like;
- by a volunteer who has experience or is willing to learn; or
- by a student who is willing to design and implement your website in order to gain experience and build his or her resume.

Some organizations hire an outside consultant to design an initial website, and then use existing staff to maintain and update the site.

A website gives you another avenue for communication with stakeholders and the general public. Promote[2] your site by:

- registering the site location (your URL or Internet address) with major search engines so that your site comes up when Internet users do a search for information using keywords that relate to your mission;
- contacting owners of related sites or similar organizations and linking to each other's websites;
- sending, by broadcast or targeted e-mail, a press release to online media outlets and appropriate e-mail lists and listservs; and
- buying banner ads on other websites.

Whether or not your organization maintains a website, consider making the Internet an active part of your community-building efforts. As with community development, often you will be building your audience one person at a time. Use the following tools for sharing information, facilitating dialogue with others, and building an audience for your site:

- Develop a list of e-mail addresses of supporters and others interested in your organization; periodically send an e-mail telling them about some aspect of the organization and its work.
- Include an e-mail gateway on your website so that visitors to the site can send you e-mail directly.
- Provide on-screen surveys and requests for information that visitors can fill out and submit directly to your organization for entry into your database.
- Track visitor connections to your site; services are available to provide you with regular usage reports to help you determine what people look at most on your site.
- Provide a forum on your site for registered visitors or the general public to read and post comments for discussion. A forum can be moderated so that only comments that have been approved by your organization show up in the discussion.
- Promote volunteer opportunities through e-mail notification or on a special section of your website.
- Set up a listserv to allow interested participants to e-mail the whole group of participants.
- Build a chat room on the site so that visitors can communicate in real time rather than with the delayed effect that listservs and e-mail generally allow.
- Make sure your street address and contact information are readily accessible on your website.

Create a privacy policy statement that adheres to the laws of your state, and make sure it is readily accessible to visitors to your site. Inform site visitors of the technology used to identify and remember visitors, and what happens with any data that is collected, including how it is used, who has access to it, and who owns it.

E-commerce

E-commerce allows you to conduct sales via your website. But remember that it requires a high level of security to ask people to use a credit card for purchases. Think carefully about your decision to conduct business online. If your organization is not already involved in product sales, consider whether there is a compelling reason to begin selling online. Make sure you have the staff resources to maintain the effort and the space to hold any merchandise and fill orders.

[2] Adapted from information found on the Benton Foundation website (*www.benton.org*).

It may be possible to subscribe to a service that provides secure online capacity for e-commerce. Compare ISPs to see if they offer e-commerce packages as part of their Web hosting services.

Online Philanthropy

The case for online philanthropy[3] is not so much that there is a huge new group of donors out there on the Web (although there may be). Rather, it recognizes that more and more people are finding out about organizations via the Internet; they are becoming more comfortable with the concept of e-commerce; donors are beginning to expect the option of contributing online; and online giving can be a low-cost way of raising funds.

If you have already decided to create a secure site for e-commerce, it may be relatively easy to add a section to allow online donations. If not, you will need to decide whether to develop internal capacity for online donations, affiliate your organization with a corporate or marketing partner, or hire out the online fundraising function to an existing organization that manages the process for a fee and/or percentage of the contributions.

Developing in-house capacity for online donations works best for large nonprofits with sizeable budgets for technology, specialized technology staff, and first-rate equipment. If you decide to go this route, make sure that your site is secure, that information will be collected in a manner compatible with your database, and that you have the staff resources to manage the function.

Affiliating with a corporate or marketing partner allows your organization to collect a percentage of the proceeds of online sales by people who are recognized as having been driven to the purchase site by your organization. *For example,* you may suggest on your website that if visitors are interested in purchasing certain items from a seller who gives a percentage of profits to your organization, they should click on a link that drives them to that seller. The seller keeps track of purchases from people who connected to them from your site and sends you a check when your percentage proceeds reach a certain level.

Hiring out your online fundraising to an organization that specializes in raising funds via the Internet is probably the easiest way to begin to accept online contributions. Most of these organizations will charge an initial fee and/or a percentage of the donations that they collect for you. It is a good idea to check with the Charity Review Council to learn more about the service you are considering. Before signing on with such an organization, consider:

- whether you need to register in other states or whether the collecting organization is registered as a professional fundraiser in every state necessary for soliciting funds online (your state attorney general can give you an opinion);
- who issues the receipt to the donor (and whether the process is clear to donors);
- whether you can control what the organization will say about your organization; and
- who owns the data about the donors.

Philanthropy via the Internet will continue to evolve as more organizations try to make use of the technology and learn from their experiences. While the possibilities are exciting, any decision to engage in online philanthropy should be considered carefully as part of a strategic planning process that considers all of the technology issues your organization faces.

[3]Adapted from the "E-commerce and Nonprofits" presentation by Chris Sullivan of the Minnesota Council of Nonprofits (*www.mncn.org*).

MANAGING CHANGE

CHAPTER 13

Managing Change

Change has become a constant in our lives. Our economy, communities, families, and organizations are making their way through turbulence, excitement, opportunity, and stress. We need to learn and grow continuously in order to keep up with this changing environment and to be prepared to cope with the positive and negative consequences of change.

As leaders in the nonprofit sector, executive directors have to find ways to manage through tumult and keep their organizations moving forward. We believe, as noted in Peter Senge's *The Dance of Change*, that "leadership actually grows from the capacity to hold creative tension, the energy generated when people articulate a vision and tell the truth (to the best of their ability) about current reality." But how do leaders recognize opportunities for change and manage change that is thrust upon their organizations? In this chapter, we explore the effects of change and the role of the executive director in helping the people in an organization accept, work through, and adapt creatively to change.

The Executive Director's Role

Change is occurring constantly – whether incremental or monumental, by design or by chance. Executive directors need to be especially vigilant about recognizing windows of opportunity for qualitative, large-scale change.

All aspects of an organization are in constant motion. The executive director has to help staff visualize the ideal state in juxtaposition with the current state. He or she then must help create a path toward the ideal state, recognizing, of course, that the ideal is never reached – it is always a process along a path. The field may have changed dramatically by the time original milestones are reached. The executive director and staff need to be constantly rethinking and retooling (See Chapter 5, **Strategic Planning and Thinking**.) The leader's role is to challenge staff to think critically and generate ideas that meet current needs while bringing the organization closer to its ideal state.

Precursors to Change

Systemic change happens when an organization creates or is confronted by circumstances that require that it either change or risk stagnation, or worse. The executive director must learn to recognize precursors to change and manage through them.

When members of an organization are not happy in their work and really want to change – but are afraid of what it means to change – they will often amplify their problems through bickering, gossip, whining, working against the leadership, and blaming. Recognize that organizations in battle with themselves do not feel fulfilled in their current state. Resist the tendency to look for a culprit – a person or group of people – to blame for these manifestations of the need for, and fear of, change. Blaming can delay the whole change process, sometimes for years. Understand that this type of organizational distress is actually energy that can be used to push change forward.

Resist, too, the inclination to simply try to stop the behaviors. Acknowledge that attempting to put a cap on this kind of distress will not stop the process; the behavior will show up in other forms. It is better to let the issues surface and be dealt with openly. Challenge the notion that leaders are successful only when they control a calm ship from one point to another. Understand that executive directors are not in control. The larger system is in control and an insightful leader will help that system grow and change in healthy directions. Recognize that there is a natural cycle of decline and renewal.

Other precursors to change include sudden events such as a huge influx of new money, a dramatic loss of funding, or a change in leadership, as well as slow burners that create growing tension that eventually reaches a crisis point; for example, no raises for staff for several years in a row.

Recognizing the Need for Change

If you notice that the same conversations are recurring again and again or that the staff is creating "disorder" because they see the need for change, it is time to ask the deeper questions about what underlying issues are causing these negative symptoms. *The greatest tension between the ideal state and the current state exists during times of crisis. That is the best time to work to define a renewing vision of the ideal state for the organization.*

The role of the leader is to help structure and discipline the organization to think critically and analyze situations before they grow out of control. Executive directors should encourage the disciplines required for a healthy view of change, such as raising questions, holding honest dialogue and open discussions, and thinking strategically.

Practices to Help the Executive Director Recognize the Need for Change

- Continually seek the opinions of staff, consumers, board members, and funders. The more you hear, even if you don't always agree, the more you learn about the opinions of others. The more people feel that their views are acknowledged, the less likely they will be to work against you and the more likely they will be to partner with you in recognizing the need for change and exploring new paths for the organization.
- Use conversations to allow people to tell their "stories," but emphasize the importance of truth-telling. Leaders should understand that different truths or realities can coexist. Your job is to bring to light conflicting realities, explore the differences in people's perspectives, and help staff and board align closely around the mission and vision of the organization.
- Ask the hard questions. For example, when change is thrust upon you by a loss of funding, ask the tougher questions. Does this program still serve its purpose? Is there energy here that can be used to significantly change the organization? Are we stagnating? Is it time to consider a merger? Should we close down the organization or the program in question?
- Try to get to a place of excruciating honesty, no matter how difficult it is. Sometimes an objective third party can help the executive director gain perspective. A wise executive director will recognize that he or she, no matter how good, is still a part of the system and may not be able to see what the whole system needs.

Helping the System to Change

The role of a leader is to help the whole system see where it wants to go, how it wants to get there, and what values it will uphold along the way. Sometimes it is helpful to have a consultant come in to help the organization work through the change process. The executive director or consultant should use conversations, skillful discussion, and agreement on future goals to align the system, including staff, board, and other stakeholders, around the mission of the organization. The objective should be to reach a set of commitments and agreements, including the following:

- Align staff around mission, vision, and program by creating a mission screen for your organization.
- Encourage and facilitate strategic thinking. Strategic thinking is a valuable methodology for the kind of visioning, programming, evaluating, relearning, and retooling that you will need to do during a change process.
- Incorporate people practices that empower staff to think, question, make decisions, and learn.
- Reflect and evaluate honestly. Creation, decline, and renewal are all part of the natural cycle. Smart directors are simply more proactive within these cycles; they name and manage them instead of allowing natural forces to wreak havoc upon the organizations they serve.
- Understand that fundraising and financial management should be completely integrated with program development and management. Recognize that each part of the organization affects the whole.

Case Study: Managing Major Change

The Six Step Program

The names and place have been omitted to protect the innocent, but the following is a real case study in managing change. The words are those of an executive director who recently led a significant organizational change process.

Once upon a time, an interim director was hired into a million-dollar, neighborhood-based multi service organization. The agency was $120,000 in debt and staff were quitting en masse as a result of five years of poor hiring of, and therefore lack of substantive leadership from, executive directors. The staff /board relationship was characterized by anger, gossip, hurt and distrust. Services were being provided inconsistently and without a uniform service delivery approach. For several years, there had been no effective outreach or communication with a community that had once wholeheartedly supported the organization but was now questioning its usefulness and ability to provide quality service.

The board had recently terminated the contract of an executive director who had pretty much run the organization into the ground. It was too little, too late. The staff was already decimated by resignations and those who remained did not trust that the board could make decisions that were good for the agency. The board (remember, these were community volunteers) felt overwhelmed; having just been through a difficult termination, they felt betrayed by the staff departures and by the knowledge they were not trusted. They felt that the remaining staff were "out-of-control" and "spoiled."

The board of directors felt they had to get the upper hand and stop staff complaints. They hired an interim director with a control and compliance philosophy. In a time when communication and healing was needed, this was the wrong "fix." More turnover of staff resulted. The board was forced to terminate the interim director.

The board was now at its wits' end and considering closing the organization. In absolute desperation, they put out a cry for help to their statewide association. They did not know that asking for help was the door-opener to a new era. *This request for help and admission that they lacked control was the first step in the change process.*

The board ended up hiring another interim (me), and I eventually decided to stay on as the permanent executive director. My first task was to get people to see that only together would we begin to find answers and change. The lesson here is that if you really value the mission and clients versus "winning" then get out of the us/them mentality when, or if you are smart, before, a crisis emerges. It is okay to admit you are powerless in this situation and that you need help. But you must find help in the right place; an organization in crisis needs the steady hand of a secure, seasoned, basically altruistic leader. This leader should have a clear idea of his or her role as a change agent.

In a crisis, a good change agent is not going to agree with one side or the other; this is very important to remember. Board members should not seek executive directors who simply parrot their positions and executive directors should not seek consultants who simply reinforce their style.

A good change agent will be arrogant enough to think change is possible and humble enough to know it takes the whole community to create change.

The second step in change is to challenge the community to join the primary change agent(s) to engage in the process.

People in crisis-ridden organizations need to be put to the test with questions such as: Who really wants to break the vicious cycle? Who is brave enough to voice the current reality? Who can bring people together to envision a new future together?

If you are too much a part of the problem, consider leaving. In a change process you must be both the changer and the changed. If you can be neither you should move out of the way.

3

The third step in the change process is to work with people through conversation to identify the current reality.

When I first arrived at the agency I did the following things (among many others like putting out fires in finance) and I suggest them as a means of building support for change:

- Meet with people individually and give them the space to tell the story of what has gone wrong with the agency from their own perspective. Ask them what they believe are the future goals and vision for the agency.
- Build some basic trust with the staff by giving them amnesty from hearsay about who they are, how they act, how they do their jobs.
- Build trust and skills by asking staff for what they think solutions are to day-to-day issues, and act on their recommendations (the beginning of incremental change).

4

The fourth step is to build consensus around a shared future.

We held an all-day, all-staff retreat about eight weeks after I arrived. I engaged the staff in group storytelling–but at the systems level to get staff to use less of an us/them approach in their analysis and to see where larger-scale systems had broken down. They were able to move back in history and see that the seeds for the problems of the last few years were actually planted when the founder left the organization in the mid 1990s. The organization did not do enough good planning around the transition, nor did the board understand how to look at the leadership needs of the organization in the context of the departure of a charismatic leader. This is why it is so important to do succession planning for both the board and the management team.

5

The fifth step is to facilitate the department of those who do not agree with the shared vision or who are unable to change.

There will be turnover when real change occurs; ideally, people who cannot get with the program will self-select out, at both the board and staff levels. Unfortunately, this is only an ideal. Executive directors managing change processes need to guide staff in defining the shared cultural commitments to the program and to the workplace. A structure of check in, feedback, or evaluation will make it clear over time who cannot uphold commitments; the executive director must name this and ask those people to leave. I did the following:

- had staff talk through and develop uniform standards of service delivery and a code of ethics;
- held staff accountable to their own expectations around service delivery and ethics; and
- managed the turnover needed for the organization to be healthy, and moved particularly quickly with those staff who proved to be the type who thrive in dysfunction and could not bring themselves to be a part of positive change.

6

The sixth step is to build capacity for quick-cycle learning and change in response to community and client needs.

This takes a long time if you are working with a staff that traditionally has had little say or power over their work. One needs to continually connect them with the core purpose of their work, typically by asking them to develop responses to the question: We do this work; so what? When asked to fill the patriarchal role and answer all the questions, throw the questions back at staff. Get them to think critically. Teach them to think about the large systems impacting their work – not just at strategic planning time, but every day. Within a year or so, magically, you will be a leader among leaders; the changed among the changers.

Helping the Staff and Board Accept Change

As you weave the various threads that will bring your organization closer to its ideal state, you may find that some people consistently fall outside of the agreements and commitments that are being reached within the organization. Some people may feel uncomfortable with change or unable to understand it. It is the executive director's job to help these individuals – whether staff or board members, and without judging them to be right or wrong – recognize that they may not have enough of a commitment to the new vision to continue with the organization. This does not mean that you should eliminate diversity of opinion or disagreement; this can be a very fine line. Sometimes a person who is making it uncomfortable for others may be raising exactly the right questions that an organization should be dealing with at a particular time. It is the executive director's job to juggle the conversational balls and call the questions that maintain alignment and push the vision forward.

It may be the executive director who is out of step with the changes taking place in the organization. If you find yourself in this situation and begin wondering if it's time to leave, initiate a conversation with your board chair or trusted peers. You may be right – but you also may be overreacting. Do a reality check, but be prepared to take the next step if your concerns are validated.

Practical Considerations for the Change Process

Organizations should allow at least 12 to 18 months for planning to result in change. Understand that there will be an impact on current processes while the organization is moving toward new programming and its resultant effects on future funding and financial management. This is strategic management at its best – bringing together future programming scenarios and staffing patterns with funding and financial considerations – and making it all work.

It can be difficult to manage finances in a change process. Staff may need more time out for meetings; the board may need to be redeveloped around a particular set of issues; you may not want to commit significant funds to a program that is in question; and you may need to hire consultants. In addition, you may be balancing the financial results of the process with the process itself.

Classic Patterns of Change

In the fifth stage of growth (see the sidebar on Karl Mathiasen's **Organizational Life Cycles: Revisited**), an organization moves strongly back toward its founding mission but with a clear understanding of the need for the systems, delegation and democratic decision making and collaboration that were called for in the earlier stages of growth. With experience, an executive director will come to understand the stage of growth the organization is in and how the tensions that are created within it can be "fixed" by the next stage. Growth stages can be seen as more spiral than circular.

Organizational Life Cycles: Revisited[1]

Organizations move through distinguishable life cycles-or stages of development-as they mature and grow. Each stage requires a different management style and organizational structure; what worked in one stage does not work in another. In fact, the management solutions of one phase often become the problems of the next.

Nonprofits are well aware of the need to adapt to changing external factors, such as funding cutbacks, new political realities, or shifting community needs. They generally don't realize, however, that they must also make periodic adjustments in response to their own internal evolution. As organizations pass from one cycle to the next, they must reassess the way they operate and make organizational changes that suit each new stage of development.

There are four typical stages that most nonprofit organizations pass through as they mature and grow. Each stage contains a relatively calm period of growth that ends with dislocation or crisis, when the organization finds that it has outgrown its old mode of operation. For example, a group that has operated in an informal, family style hits a crisis when it can no longer coordinate the efforts of its growing staff. It responds by instituting

[1]Karl Mathiasen of the Management Assistant Group, Washington, D.C. can be reached by telephone at 202-238-7587 or by email at: MAGMail@msn.com.

centralized management with more formalized procedures. That solution, however, can eventually lead to a new crisis: a reaction against the constrictions of top-down management and demands for more delegation of authority and decentralization of tasks. Each new stage is thus influenced by the previous one. Management's response to each crisis period will largely determine how successfully a group moves into the next phase.

Phase I: Informal In their early years, nonprofits are characterized by intense creativity and commitment. Their founders are usually highly entrepreneurial and passionately committed to the organization's goals. They attract a few other highly committed people who jump into long hours of work, rewarded not by status or money, but by the satisfaction of advancing the cause.

Thus, the group focuses on mission and programs. Organizational structure and management style are relaxed, normal, and individualistic. Roles and responsibilities are loosely defined and often overlap. Communication among staff is frequent and fluid, and they feel like one big family – in which everyone is a part of everything.

This flexibility and informality are essential to the young organization's ability to establish itself. Yet these very features contain the seeds of future problems. As the organization grows, informal, sporadic communication becomes inadequate. New employees seem to be less fiercely dedicated and motivated than those who were there from the start. A loose management style is no longer sufficient to assure accountability and satisfactory communication or to guarantee high performance and productivity. Founders discover they can no longer rely on charisma and cause to keep the organization running. They find themselves burdened with management responsibilities and demands for more structure and clarity. At the same time, fears of bureaucracy begin to surface, particularly among the original staff who long for the good old days when people worked independently, with little direction, and were not constrained by rules, systems, and procedures.

At this point, a crisis of leadership occurs. The organization needs stronger management, but creative founders classically are neither interested in nor temperamentally suited to provide this kind of managerial direction. At the same time, it's difficult for them to let go of their "baby" and allow the organization to bring in new, more effective management staff.

Phase II: Structured The organization typically gets past this crisis by introducing more structure and tighter management. Job descriptions are written, performance standards and expectations are clarified, and supervisory lines are clearly defined. Personnel policies and a variety of other operational policies and procedures are written and standardized. The organizational structure becomes more centralized, and staff responsibilities are divided in more focused, specialized, and confined ways. Gone are the days of being one big family, in which everyone is involved in everything. Top management adopts a significantly more directive style, communication becomes more formal and impersonal, and authority is increasingly centralized.

These structures and systems are a necessary adjustment to growth and to Phase I's informality, but they, too, bring with them the seeds of a crisis that will propel the organization into yet another phase of development. Control becomes too centralized, procedures too rigid, hierarchy too cumbersome, and participation too limited. The staff's sense of investment and ownership wane and they do not have enough freedom to carry out responsibilities effectively on their own. Initiative and creativity become stifled. Eventually, a crisis erupts-this time a crisis of control characterized by demands for more autonomy and for greater staff input into decision making. To get beyond this crisis, most groups have to move toward a greater delegation of responsibility and authority. However, this is often very difficult for the group's top managers, whose style has been to direct and control, not to let go, guide, and coordinate. Often a leadership transition becomes necessary at this point.

Phase III: Decentralization As management functions become decentralized, the organization typically experiences a burst of initiative and growth, expanding into new issues, approaches, projects, and areas of activity. Most plans and decisions are made at the project or departmental level, with the executive director or other top central managers intervening only when serious problems arise. In fact, most staffers have infrequent communication with the top managers.

Extensive delegation has made rapid growth possible, but it also leads to a new set of problems. Top management loses control over highly diversified and compartmentalized operations. Fiefdoms develop, little communication or cross-fertilization occur, coordination breaks down, and internal competition for funding, which too often escalates into turf battles, is common. "Projectitis" becomes rampant, with each separate unit focusing on its own interests and goals rather than on the overall purpose of the organization. As a result, increasing calls begin to be heard for greater cohesiveness, coordination, integration, and a renewed sense of connectedness and unified direction.

Phase IV: Consolidation In order to achieve greater coherence, consistency, and coordination, the organization redefines its structure to consolidate and integrate programs and to institute cross-cutting team approaches. The authority of central managers is strengthened, formal planning processes are introduced and institutionalized, and structures and systems are developed for coordinated planning, closer communication, and frequent staff reporting.

This greater emphasis on coordination, accountability, and planning can lead to a red tape crisis, which occurs when proliferating meetings, processes, and systems begin to make more work than they facilitate, The challenge thus becomes striking the right balance between overall focus, central planning and direction, on the one hand, and staff freedom, creativity, and effectiveness, on the other.

Mentoring the Executive Director

The capacity for understanding complex situations matures over time. Most people could benefit from mentors or advisors, but less seasoned executive directors would benefit greatly from a more seasoned mentor, within the sector, that they admire and can learn from. All executive directors, but especially those new to the job, should actively seek to establish relationships with people who can act as sounding boards, help clarify situations, and give advice on what direction to take.

Isolation is a classic problem for executive directors. Among other things, it can distort perspective. Talk to people – the staff, board, clients, funders, and people in the community. Talk to your mentors. Allow others to help you to change and grow and remain self-aware – and best meet the challenges of leading a change process.

Continuous Learning

Most people assume that the executive director of an organization is completely aligned with its mission. Reflect on your beliefs and your own personal mission. Are you aligned with an organization that will move you forward in your own life's mission? If not, it will be difficult to provide the strength of leadership that will be needed to carry the organization forward through change. People will be depending on you to act as a role model and to share your knowledge, your skill set, your experience, and your passion. Leadership requires a commitment to yourself, to others, and to the organization; it requires self-awareness, openness to criticism, continuous learning, and growth.

APPENDIX

APPENDIX

Sample Organizational Assessment Tool

This tool is not inclusive; it is a sample. Asking questions such as the following will help a new executive director become oriented to the health of the organization. As much as possible, use this as a guide in conducting real conversations with individuals or groups made up of staff, board members, and other stakeholders.

Mission, vision, and planning

1. What is your understanding of the agency's mission? Do you believe there is a common understanding of this mission?
2. What is your understanding of the agency's core values?
3. Do you feel these values are lived out on a day-to-day basis? That is, do people behave in a way that is consistent with the values? If not, why not?

4. Do you believe the agency's programs are in line with the mission, and work to fulfill it?
5. Is there a commonly held vision for the agency?
6. Do you believe staff see themselves as part of one large system–and that each of us is responsible for the success and failures of this larger system?
7. Who do you think staff feel most accountable to? Who do you feel accountable to? Do you believe the board and others in the organization feel accountable to those in whose name they do business (our clients, constituents, consumers)?
8. What is your vision for the agency? The program you are a part of?
9. Is this vision translated into a strategic plan? If there is no plan, do you think the organization is strategic anyway? If so, how?
10. Who developed the plan? Was the process inclusive? Did staff have a voice? Did constituents? If not, why not?

Structure and systems

11. Could you describe the organizational structure?
12. Do you understand where and how decisions are made within the agency?
13. Does the decision-making process include those doing the actual work?
14. Are there clear processes for communication between individual staff members? Among program staff members? Between teams? Among management team members? Between the executive director and the staff? The executive director and the board? The board and the staff?
15. Are there issues with communication? If so, how would you characterize the breakdowns?
16. What are the board's major responsibilities?
17. What are the executive director's major responsibilities?
18. Is there any confusion in role between the board (governance) and the executive director (management)?
19. Is there a method by which staff interests are fairly represented to the board?
20. Is there consistent supervision and evaluation? If so, what does it look like?

Supporting functions

21. Do you know how funds are raised for the agency? Do you have any new ideas for generating funds/income? Do you have any concerns about our fundraising efforts or practices?
22. Do you understand how money is managed here? Do you feel there are adequate checks and balances? Do you have any concerns about how money is managed?
23. Can you describe how evaluation of programs happens? Does the evaluation process tell you anything about how our programs are working for the people they were intended for?
24. Do you believe we are in the public eye enough? How would you describe the effectiveness of our marketing, public relations–communication practices with various stakeholders, particularly the community and constituents?
25. Where do you see the organization in three years? What barriers might keep our system from getting to this vision?
26. What are the three most urgent concerns you have about the organization?
27. What are the areas of greatest satisfaction you have about the organization?
28. Are we ethical in all that we do?

Exercise 1: VISIONING THE FUTURE

Time: at least 90 minutes

Directions: The session leader splits the larger group into small groups of five or six people, making sure that each group has a good mix of people from different teams or departments, especially if it is a large agency. Have each group pick a facilitator to keep the conversation focused, a recorder, and a reporter.

The charge of each group is to imagine the organization as it will be five (or 10) years from now. Each person will imagine the future organization that he or she most wants to create. The group will then take the various future images and come up with a shared, preferred vision that is realistic.

Steps:

1. Allow individuals time on their own to sort through some of the following questions as a guide to describing the organization.
2. After this time for thinking, give each person a chance to speak to each question. Capture the highlights of the conversation either by recording notes on big paper or by drawing a picture of what the organization looks like.

Questions: You can write your own questions to help guide people in developing a future image of the organization or have people discuss responses to all or some of the questions listed below. You may want to encourage the use of art as a tool for expression, through drawing a vision, putting on a skit, creating a song, or writing a poem.

- Who will the stakeholders of this organization be five years from now?
- How will we work with them?
- How will we produce value for them, or what are the outcomes for them from being involved with us?
- What will be the strongest trends influencing our work, our clients, and our community?
- What will our image be in the community?
- What will be the impact of our work?
- How will we gather money to do what we do?
- What will our facilities look like?
- How will the staff working in the facilities look (happy, stressed, diverse)?
- What have we done to ensure the future of our organization for our community?

Next steps:

1. The session leader reconvenes the large group. Each small group should be prepared to highlight their conversations or present their artwork to the larger group. The facilitator should note the similarities that emerge in the group's descriptions of the future.
2. The facilitator synthesizes the findings or asks the group to highlight and describe the similarities.
3. The session leader asks a small group to continue synthesizing the vision into one draft vision statement.
4. The session leader tests the vision statement with the full staff and board, edits it, and incorporates it in places where it will be a visual reminder of the future that people are trying to reach collectively.

Exercise 2: VALUES ALIGNMENT

Time: 90 minutes

Setting: This exercise (or other versions of it) is typically used at retreats, where the organization is represented by a wide variety of individuals, including board members, staff, and sometimes others.

Step 1: "What I value most . . ."

From a list of values that has been supplied (using a very inclusive list of both work and personal values), ask people to select individually the 10 values that are most important to them. People can add any values of their own to this list.

Step 2: Elimination

Have folks imagine that they are only permitted to have five values. Which five are they willing to give up? Have them cross the rejected values off their list. Then have them cross off one more, bringing the list of values to four; then have them cross off another one, bringing the list to three.

Step 3: Articulation

Ask participants to pair off with another person in the room. Then, have each person take a turn answering the following questions:

- What are your top three values, and why are these the most important to you?
- Would your life be different if these values were prominent and practiced (or are they already)?
- Are these values reflected in our workplace today? Should they be? (Keep in mind that not all personal values can be translated into work values.)

Then ask each individual in each pair to answer the following question:

- If there is one value out of the top three that I would want articulated in the workplace, which one is it?

Step 4: Creating the list of workplace values

After each person has identified the one value he or she would like articulated in the workplace, list the choices on big paper.

Ask the group: If we look at this list, which values could we agree to uphold as a group? Are there other values (that are not on the current list) that we could agree to uphold? Add the additional values to the big paper.

Step 5: Prioritizing five values for the current time

Give participants five dots (or choose a different number) and ask them to vote for the values they most want to see articulated in the workplace. People can put all their dots on one value or spread them out.

Step 6: Turning values into behaviors that can be upheld–the real work

A value is just a word unless it is put into action. If clients could see staff living their values, what would the behaviors in the workplace look like? What would the board, the community, or the funders see? If the board was living the values of the organization, what would the staff, clients, funders, and community see in action?

Talk through and write down the behavior or indicator that would demonstrate that the values the group chooses are alive and well in the organization.
For example:

Value	Behavior
Honesty	Truth-telling; no talking behind people's backs
Youth Empowerment	Access for youth in the planning and design of programs
Service	All requests for information answered within 24 hours
Respect	Phone calls returned promptly; people on time for meetings; deadlines met

Sample Board Member Job Description

Title: Board Member

Contact Person: Chairperson or Executive Director

Purpose: A member of the (name of organization) board of directors is an integral part of the leadership team, providing direction and vision for (name of organization). He or she is responsible, together with the full board of directors, for governance and oversight of all aspects of (name of organization). Key responsibilities are governance and promoting the mission of (name of organization).

Requirements/Skills:

1. Commitment to the mission of (name of organization).
2. Ability to work with other people.
3. Willingness to make the required time commitment.
4. Commitment to the financial well-being of (name of organization), including oversight of the budget and fundraising process, making an annual contribution to the organization, and participating in at least one fundraising event each year.
5. Commitment to encouraging staff development.
6. Ability to maintain confidentiality.
7. Willingness to be regularly accessible by telephone or other means.

Responsibilities:

1. Attendance at all meetings of the board of directors.
2. Participation in at least one fundraising or other major organizational event each year.
3. Attendance at workshops, board training, and any other special meetings that are scheduled.
4. Promotion of the mission and goals of (name of organization) in the community.
5. Service on a board committee.

Resources:

1. Board manual
2. Readings on board development
3. Board training, as needed

Minimum Time Commitment:

1. Two-year term
2. Two to three hours of preparation and meeting time per board meeting
3. Five hours total work per month

Results:

1. Development of leadership skills
2. An efficient, accountable organization
3. Contribution to the very important cause of (mission of organization)

Sample Board Member Code of Ethics

As a Board Member of (*name of organization*), I understand that I am here to serve the clients, community, and staff of the organization through the expectations outlined in the board member job description.

I understand that I am not to use my role as a board member:

___ for financial gain for myself or a relative

___ to advance a personal agenda or meet a personal need

___ to be in "control" of the organization or its employees

I understand that my role is one of stewardship. As a steward of this agency's mission and overall viability, I seek open dialogue with other key stakeholders, including staff, clients, volunteers, funders, and community members. I will use (and can expect to be taught through a board development process) dialogue and skillful discussion in conversations about the agency's business, policies, values, or future direction. I understand that I am part of an ongoing process of growth and learning, as are all other stakeholders in the agency.

I understand that my solutions may not be the only, or the right, solutions for this agency, but know that raising questions that bring the group to mutually agreed upon directions and actions is expected of me.

If problems or concerns arise, I will address these openly, within the organization's communication protocols.

I will respect the organization's mutually agreed upon values and mission and make all decisions within the context of mission and values.

____

Signed Dated

Sample Conflict of Interest Statement for Board Members

As a member of the board of (name of organization), I pledge to act in the best interest of those in whose name the organization does business, including our clients, constituents, and community members. I will keep confidential any information that is meant to be so. I understand that my role is to act as part of a collective decision-making body and to work collaboratively towards shared decisions. I carry the authority of the board only within the context of the full board or with the express authority of the full board. My efforts are made with the intent of furthering the mission of the organization, not my personal needs or goals. The governance role is not to be used for financial gain or personal advantage by me or my family, friends, or associates. My responsibility is to support the needs, goals, and vision of the organization and the people for whom it exists.

Human Resources Development Matrix

A human resources development matrix can be used as part of an orientation review process for a new employee. This sample provides space to list the supervisor or organizational responsibilities for providing specific support to a new employee.

Competency Matrix: Employee Engagement in the Workplace

Competencies Expected of All Employees	How Well Competencies Are Attained	Supervisory/Organizational Support for Employee in Attaining Competencies
Understands the mission and can reflect organizational values that underscore the mission and purpose		
Understands the history of the organization and its current structure, including the role of the board of directors. Has met with the executive director or a board member to discuss the mission and values. Has attended a board meeting.		
Understands what the agency considers to be the root causes of issues that bring consumers to our doors (poverty, economics, social, or psychological issues). Understands and can articulate the analysis of our shared situation with consumers.		
Understands the agency's way of doing things within the "field," and its philosophy of service delivery – documented with a reading list and meetings with the team and an individual supervisor, and demonstrated in day-to-day interaction with consumers and coworkers.		
Understands how the philosophy of service delivery extends to the methods of service delivery that we employ. Can list key methods and describe how he or she learned about them, whether through cross-training, observation, supervisor instruction, etc.		
Understands funding streams and sources and our obligations under particular contracts. Has met with development staff once for an overview during the first six months.		
Understands the overview of the agency budget and the workings of the departmental budget. Has met and received an overview from finance staff during the first six months.		
Understands the agency's outreach and education component. Has attended at least one outside engagement during the first six months.		

Competency Matrix: Employee Engagement in the Workplace (continued)

Competencies Expected of All Employees	How Well Competencies Are Attained	Supervisory/Organizational Support for Employee in Attaining Competencies
Understands how the agency evaluates itself and its programs. Participates in this evaluation by maintaining basic data and raising critical questions.		
Understands the overall planning process and his or her role in it.		
Understands office and program procedures, as well as the decorum that should be observed.		
Understands and uses information systems well, including: • confidentiality protocols; • telephone protocols; • mail protocols, such as when to send letters signed with own name, etc.; • appropriate uses of e-mail; • computer protocols if shared, filing systems, confidentiality, etc.; • data required by this position; • financial information, including timekeeping and reporting, etc.; and • reports required by this position. Has viewed training videos and read through required reading.		
Has been trained in what constitutes good supervision and evaluation; how we define organization-wide accountability and accountability to other stakeholders, such as consumers, the community, funders, and the public; and how our system works.		
Has the capacity to understand and work toward using systems thinking in problem-solving.		

Notes

Notes

Notes

Notes